Rate cards
hose
kpps Printing

Legal Almanac Series No. 24
A *completely new title*

Voting
and
Election Laws

Laws for Voters
by
Constance E. Smith, Ph.D
Eagleton Institute of Politics

(This completely original work replaces
"Election Laws")

Oceana Publications, Inc.

80 Fourth Ave.   **New York 3, N. Y.**

324.73
SM 5v
40177
October, 1960

DEDICATION

To my mother and father

Library of Congress Catalog Card Number: 60-7367

Manufactured in the United States of America

TABLE OF CONTENTS

Chapter 1

Chapter 2

Chapter 3

Chapter 4

Appendix

ACKNOWLEDGMENTS

The completion of any work for publication is inevitably a cooperative effort, and this volume is no exception. Although neither has been directly consulted on this work, I want first to acknowledge my debt to Miss Louise Overacker, Professor of Political Science, Emeritus at Wellesley College and to Professor Arthur N. Holcombe, Professor of Government at Harvard University, whose teaching and writings stimulated my initial interest in electoral legislation. This particular study of voting and registration laws was undertaken and completed under the auspices of the Eagleton Institute at Rutgers—the State University of New Jersey, and I am especially indebted to Mr. Donald G. Herzberg, Executive Director of the Institute, for his encouragement and help. Mrs. Anne Siegel of the Eagleton staff has been of inestimable assistance at every stage of the research and writing, and other members of the staff have willingly contributed their comments and secretarial skills for which I am very grateful. Miss Eleanor R. Webster deserves profound thanks for her thorough and intelligent editing of the final manuscript. Needless to say, the full responsibility for any contentions expressed and any errors committed rests with the author, who stands ready to accept the suggestions and corrections of interested readers.

New Brunswick, New Jersey
February, 1960

This completely original volume by one of the country's most informed political analysts replaces the earlier volume 24 in the LEGAL ALMANAC SERIES. *Legal Almanacs attempt to bring the law on various subjects to the layman in non-technical language. These books do not take the place of your attorney's advice, but they serve to introduce you to your legal rights and responsibilities.*

THE PUBLISHER

Chapter 1

THE RIGHT TO VOTE

The right to vote is of signal importance in the United States where the governmental system depends on the consent which the governed give to those who govern. In a democracy the vote determines who the leaders will be and what direction their leadership will take; thus an election is perhaps the most crucial confrontation between the people and their government. The right of each citizen to cast a ballot, although now taken for granted in the United States, is the inheritance of centuries of class struggle and bitter fighting between the rulers and the people in the various countries of the world whose influence has shaped America. Nor should the recency of the struggle's culmination in our own country be overlooked—universal suffrage became a fact rather than a battlecry of the suffragettes a bare forty years ago when the adoption of the 19th Amendment extended the franchise to women. But the mere existence of the constitutional privilege to vote, or to go to the polls, is not enough. To be effective, voting must be protected by safeguards which insure the independence of the voter as well as the integrity of his vote. Without such safeguards a suffrage right is meaningless. Yet in any social process as complex as an election, involving the highest stakes of power and status, participants will inevitably attempt to subvert the procedure and the results to private interests and goals. And, in fact, every election year does reveal scattered instances of corruption and dishonesty; the number of such illegalities has decreased so markedly in recent years, however, that today it can fairly be claimed that American election results are on the whole free from serious distortion due to chicanery or downright fraud.

A voter can hardly be said to have a voting privilege if because of intimidation—whether by public officials, private groups or social pressure—he is afraid to express his honest choice on a ballot. A meaningful privilege requires that a ballot is cast in secrecy and counted anonymously, and extensive state legislation provides for these essential conditions in all national and state elections and in nearly all local elections. In addition, the voter must be protected against corruption and the deliberate distortion of electoral results. Today carefully-drawn registration requirements ensure that the voter is the person he claims to be, and stringent legal limitations on election officials and detailed descriptions of their functions and the procedures to be followed at every stage of the election process guarantee the accurate recording and counting of each vote. Futhermore, unless a voter is to be merely a rubber-stamp who goes to the polls to confirm preselected candidates, he must be presented with a ballot which lists genuine choices of candidates from which he may make his selection. It is precisely this choice which distinguishes free democratic elections from elections in a totalitarian society; the latter are essentially exercises in the expression of loyalty to a single slate of "candidates" hand-picked by the ruling group. Since the presentation of alternatives is one of the major functions of our American political parties, it is of considerable importance that state election codes contain innumerable laws aimed at encouraging and protecting the proper operation of party machinery in the United States.

If the voter requires protection, so too does the society —protection from participation by the irrational, the unintelligent or the irresponsible in electoral decisions on public matters and popular leaders. In all states the idiot, the insane and the criminal are prohibited from registering to vote, and paupers and inmates of charitable institutions are usually disfranchised lest they be tempted to sell their vote or cast it for personal gain rather than public good. Other voting qualifications are imposed: a mature age, in some cases the ability to read and write, a period of residence in the community and in some types of elections (usually those which involve decisions on the expenditure of public money), property ownership. All of these requirements are intended to enfranchise an electorate which will be capable of arriving at sound decisions on public questions.

The structure of the American electoral system derives from our federal system of government, with its legal distribution of power between the central government and the various state governments. The Constitution delineates these spheres of national and state authority, and it is of far-reaching significance in the development of our system of elections that the states rather than the national government were assigned major responsibility for elections. The scattered references to electors and elections in the Constitution, when taken together, suggest the general pattern of American elections; but this skeleton is filled out by literally thousands of state laws which comprise the definitive legislation on every phase of voting, party organization, campaign procedures, nominations, and elections. The fifty state systems vary considerably since each state legislature is virtually autonomous in enacting election laws; thus one must piece together the specific provisions for each state to form a comprehensive picture of the American electoral system.

Constitutional Provisions

Certain constitutional provisions provide the key to the structure and development of the American electoral system. For example, the Constitution grants to the state legislatures the power to prescribe "the times, places and manner of holding elections for senators and representatives," and also the power to determine the manner of appointing presidential electors. These two grants of power coupled with each state's unquestioned authority to control all elections for state offices endow the states with decisive control over all elections; for, while it is true that the Constitution reserves to Congress the right to make or alter regulations for congressional or senatorial elections, Congress has only rarely exercised this power and then only in very limited ways. The Constitution also grants the executive in each state the power to call a special election if a vacancy occurs in congressional representation.

One reads the Constitution in vain for a concrete definition of who shall have the *right* to vote; there is only the declaration in the 15th and 19th Amendments that a citizen may not be *denied* the right to vote because of race, color, previous condition of servitude, or sex. A section of the 14th Amendment defining citizens as "all persons born or naturalized in the United States and subject to the jurisdiction thereof" is relevant, since citizenship is in all states a requisite for suffrage. With the exception of these broad restrictions, full responsibility for determining voter qualifications comes within state jurisdiction; the Constitution states that the electors for members of both the United States Senate and House of Representatives shall "have the qualifications requisite for electors of the most numerous branch of the state legislature." These are the salient constitutional sections on elections; for more specific laws on registration and voting, one must turn to state codes.

State Provisions for Voter Qualifications

For the most part, the basic qualifications for voting on which state legislation is predicated are straightforward, reasonable, and relatively simple for the average person to fulfill. They are seldom arbitrary, and are largely justifiable as logical attempts to enfranchise electors with the maturity, mental capacity and stake in the community to cast a responsible ballot. However, the patchwork quality of most state election codes, with their bewildering array of minute provisions, makes the job of isolating the basic provisions unnecessarily laborious and complicated.

CITIZENSHIP: Citizenship is an unexceptionable requirement for voting in every state. In addition to the broad provision of the 14th Amendment that a citizen is anyone born or naturalized in the United States, there are numerous laws dealing with special cases for the acquisition of citizenship. Anyone wishing to vote who is uncertain of his citizenship status should check with the Immigration and Naturalization Service of the United States Government (which has field offices in a number of major cities) to establish his exact status, since the local registrar for elections in a community is not legally qualified to determine citizenship status. Every applicant when he presents himself to the registrar must either take an oath that he is a natural-born citizen or present his original naturalization papers or a certified copy of them for the registrar's inspection before he can be registered as an elector.

AGE: Traditionally the age of 21 has come to be regarded as the mark of maturity; although there are some legal exceptions to this, only three states grant voting rights to citizens before the 21st birthday. In Georgia and Kentucky, the voting age is 18; in Alaska 19 year olds may vote. In most states, if the prospective voter will be 21 by the time of the primary or general election immediately following the registration period, he is allowed to register. And in certain states, a person under 21 may vote in the party primary, provided he will be of legal voting age by the time the general election is held.

Since the beginning of World War II there has been considerable political pressure for a constitutional amendment which would reduce the national voting age to 18. Advocates of lowering the voting age argue that a man who is old enough to face bullets is old enough to mark ballots—clearly a contention difficult to refute—but in spite of urging from the President, pressure from interested citizen groups and the introduction of several proposals for such an amendment, Congress, which would have the sole power to enact a national law establishing for all states such a revision in the voting age, has not acted. The possible political consequences of enlarging the electorate are interesting to contemplate; it was reliably estimated in 1952 that approximately one million of the three and one-half million persons in the armed forces were under 21.

RESIDENCE: Every state code sets forth residence requirements specifying the length of time one must reside in the state, the county and the election district before he can register to vote. The underlying principle is clear: the assumption that only through living in a state for at least six months can one become sufficiently conversant with local problems and candidates to vote intelligently. These requirements also prevent transients or migrants from participating in elections and possibly overruling the votes (and presumably the better judgment) of longtime residents. While acknowledging the wisdom of the principle, one should not overlook the danger of excessive residence requirements which may needlessly disfranchise otherwise qualified voters.

Most codes very carefully define "residence" for voting purposes. "Residence", in this sense, refers to one's permanent abode, to the location from which one has no present intention of moving and to which one intends to return after temporary absence. For a married man, the place where his family resides is usually considered his residence unless he and his wife are separated and maintain separate homes. For a single man, the place where he sleeps is usually regarded as his residence. One cannot have two residences for the purpose of establishing voting rights, for as soon as one place is claimed as residence, the right to claim a second is relinquished.

An elector does not lose his residence because he is temporarily absent from his home. All election codes specifically state that residence is not lost by a person who is serving in the armed forces or in service agencies connected with the armed forces; and most codes further provide that electors who are absent because they work

14

for the state or federal government, or are employed in navigation in inland waterways, or who are attending a school, college, university or other institution of learning, retain their residence rights. It should be noted, however, that just as one does not lose residence while engaged in these pursuits, neither does one acquire state residence by virtue of being stationed at a military establishment or by being a resident student within a state. This restriction does not work a hardship on military personnel, for all states now comply with federal law in providing absentee voting privileges for men in the armed forces, and usually for their wives and dependents as well. The serviceman thus votes by absentee ballot in the district where he lived prior to entering the armed forces. In most states the law declares that confinement to prison or to a charitable institution or asylum does not deprive one of residence rights, but persons confined to mental or penal institutions are not allowed to register and those in charitable institutions are almost never granted the franchise.

States may be divided into three categories with regard to residence requirements:

> REQUIRING SIX MONTHS OF RESIDENCE IN THE STATE: Idaho; Indiana; Iowa; Kansas; Maine; Michigan; Minnesota; Nebraska; Nevada; New Hampshire; New Jersey and Oregon. South Carolina grants voting rights to ministers of the gospel and their wives and public school teachers after six months of residence.

> REQUIRING TWO YEARS OF RESIDENCE IN THE STATE: Louisiana; Mississippi; and South Carolina (with the above exception).

> REQUIRING ONE YEAR OF RESIDENCE IN THE STATE: All states not listed above.

In addition to residence in the state, one must also prove that he has lived for the requisite time within a county and an election district. Such requirements range from a one year parish or county residence in Louisiana and South Carolina to 40 days in Nebraska and Ohio and

30 days in Arizona, Idaho, Kansas, Montana and Nevada, with the remaining states requiring from two to six months. District residence requirements run from 10 days in Iowa, Nebraska, Nevada, Wisconsin and Wyoming to one year in Mississippi (with an exception granted for ministers of the gospel and their wives who may vote after six months residence in the district). In 35 of the states the residence required is three months or less in the election district, and there is no requirement at all for district or precinct residence in such states as Florida, Georgia, Idaho, Montana, New Jersey, Tennessee, and West Virginia. The state-by-state summary in Table I, which gives exact requirements for each state, suggests at a glance the diversity of state regulations on residence.

Although no one would recommend abandonment of residence requirements altogether, it is often contended by responsible critics that some state regulations are overly stringent. It is estimated, for instance, that over five percent of the American voting population is unable to meet the residence requirement in most elections and the implications of such widespread disfranchisement in a democratic society cannot be ignored. One has only to look at the statistics of population movement in the United States, especially during and since the second World War, to know that the problem of disfranchisement of sizable portions of the electorate can only become more acute unless residence requirements are reduced to reasonable time limits. One partial remedy is suggested by recent laws in Connecticut, Wisconsin and California. In Connecticut, an elector who moves to another state may, for two years after he moves, vote by absentee ballot in presidential elections in the Connecticut municipality in which he lived. He enjoys this privilege only until he becomes an elector in his new state of residence. A Wisconsin statute, adopted by referendum in 1954, attacks the problem conversely, allowing residents of less than one year (the normal requirement for voting in that state) to vote in presidential elections provided they were qualified electors in their former state of residence. A still more lenient

California law provides that a person is eligible after only 54 days' residence to vote in presidential elections, provided he was a qualified voter in his former state. Although such "new registrants" must comply with special registration and voting procedures, nevertheless they are afforded opportunity to participate in national elections. In spite of Congressional recommendation, however, no other states have emulated these three in reducing residence requirements for national elections.

LITERACY: Unquestionably literacy is a desirable asset for the responsible elector; a voter who can read for himself newspaper and party information on candidates and issues need not rely on word-of-mouth recommendations or hearsay about political figures and can maintain, or so the reasoning goes, his own independent political views. As desirable as literacy is, fewer than half of the states administer literacy tests for voters, and in some of these the purpose is not constructive but is simply to provide another hurdle for the Negro registrant. Twenty states retain some check on literacy: there are nine in the North (Connecticut, Delaware, Maine, Massachusetts, New Hampshire, New York, Oregon, Washington, and Wyoming); seven in the South (Alabama, Georgia, Louisiana, Mississippi, North Carolina, South Carolina, and Virginia); two in the Southwest (Arizona and California); and the new states of Alaska and Hawaii. The exact requirements for each state are found in Chart I in the appendix.

State attempts to enfranchise only the "literate" range from a requirement that the applicant be able to read or write English or his mother tongue to one that the potential elector be able to read any section of the state or federal constitution and demonstrate that he understands it. An obvious drawback to the provisions which require a voter to show understanding or give a reasonable interpretation of a section of a constitution (as the Louisiana and Mississippi statutes require) is the difficulty of establishing fair and sound criteria for the determination of "understanding". When such evaluation falls within the discretionary power of the registrar (as it does in North

Table I

RESIDENCE REQUIREMENTS

State		County	City or Town	Precinct, Ward or District
Alabama	1 year	6 months		3 months
Alaska	1 year			30 days
Arizona	1 year	30 days		30 days
Arkansas	1 year	6 months		1 month
California	1 year[1]	90 days		54 days
Colorado	1 year	90 days	30 days	15 days
Connecticut	1 year		6 months	
Delaware	1 year	3 months		30 days
Florida	1 year	6 months		
Georgia	1 year	6 months		
Hawaii	1 year			3 months
Idaho	6 months	30 days[2]		
Illinois	1 year	90 days		30 days
Indiana	6 months		60 days	30 days
Iowa	6 months	60 days		10 days
Kansas	6 months	30 days		30 days
Kentucky	1 year	6 months		30 days
Louisiana	2 years	1 year		60 days
Maine	6 months		3 months	3 months[3]
Maryland	1 year	6 months		6 months
Massachusetts	1 year		6 months	
Michigan	6 months			30 days
Minnesota	6 months			30 days
Mississippi	2 years		1 year	1 year[4]
Missouri	1 year	60 days		60 days

State				
Montana	1 year	30 days		10 days
Nebraska	6 months	40 days		10 days
Nevada	6 months	30 days		6 months
New Hampshire	6 months			
New Jersey	6 months	60 days		30 days
New Mexico	1 year	90 days		30 days
New York	1 year		4 months	30 days
North Carolina	1 year	90 days		30 days
North Dakota	1 year	40 days		40 days
Ohio	1 year			30 days
Oklahoma	1 year	6 months		30 days
Oregon	6 months			2 months
Pennsylvania	1 year[5]			
Rhode Island	1 year		6 months	
South Carolina	2 years[6]	1 year		4 months
South Dakota	1 year[7]	90 days		30 days
Tennessee	1 year	3 months		
Texas	1 year	6 months		
Utah	1 year	4 months		60 days
Vermont	1 year		3 months	
Virginia	1 year		6 months	30 days
Washington	1 year	90 days	30 days	30 days
West Virginia	1 year	60 days[8]		
Wisconsin	1 year[1]			10 days
Wyoming	1 year	60 days		10 days

Legend

1 Special provisions for voting for presidential electors.
2 Cannot vote in county elections unless have residence of 6 months in county and 90 days in precinct.
3 Four months in municipality for municipal elections.
4 Ministers of the gospel in charge of an organized church and their wives may vote after 6 months' residence in district, but must have 2 years' residence in state.
5 Six months if previously an elector or native of the state.
6 Ministers of the gospel and public school teachers may vote after 6 months' residence.
7 Must also be resident of United States for 5 years.
8 For municipal elections, 60 days' residence in city.

Carolina where the statute declares it the duty of the registrar to "administer" the literacy tests), it is almost impossible to ensure uniform treatment of registrants throughout the state. Any evaluative system which does not contain specific standards for determining success and failure is subject to the partiality of the person giving the test. New York has evolved probably the best answer to this problem by placing literacy testing in the hands of the Board of Regents which provides an official examination that is graded objectively. The elector who cannot produce evidence of his educational attainment is required to pass such a test. In Georgia, on the other hand, the alternative test for the person who cannot read or write contains a set of 30 standard questions of which the illiterate voter must orally answer 20 in order to qualify to vote. The questions are detailed (What is the definition of a felony in Georgia? Who is the solicitor general of the State Judicial Circuit in which you live and who is the judge of such circuit? What are the names of the persons who occupy the following offices in your county: Clerk of the Superior Court, Ordinary, Sheriff?) and would seem to be extraordinarily difficult for the generally well-informed and presumably well-qualified voter to answer, to say nothing of the illiterate.

Originally literacy tests were adopted by some of the northern states (Connecticut in 1855 and Massachusetts in 1857) to prevent the voting of new immigrants who, because of their inability to read and write, were susceptible to corruption by political machines. After the adoption of the 15th Amendment in 1870, which removed color, race and previous servitude as barriers to voting, the southern states began incorporating literacy requirements into their election laws. Mississippi was the first to adopt such a law in 1890. State literacy provisions have been revised and refined from time to time, but recent years have seen little interest in new adoption of such tests in states which have not previously had them. Undoubtedly the decrease in immigration since the 1920's and the spread of compulsory public education will eventually render obsolete tests which are designed only to ascertain minimum literacy.

In the states which do not have literacy requirements, laws have been enacted to provide assistance for the illiterate elector at the polls. Usually the elector requiring assistance is aided by two election officials, one from each major party, and he is thus protected from political intimidation or undue influence. In all states which have literacy requirements except Hawaii, Louisiana, Mississippi, North Carolina, South Carolina, and Washington, the voter who is prevented from reading or writing by physical disability or blindness is either completely excused from fulfilling the requirement or is given a special examination suitable to his disability. Some of these special arrangments are described in Chapter 3.

POLL TAX: The payment of a poll tax is a prerequisite for voting in Alabama, Arkansas, Mississippi, Texas, and Virginia. The list of those who have paid the poll tax replaces a registration list in Arkansas and Texas, and in Virginia voting lists are compiled from poll tax records. While it is true that the tax is not exorbitant (the annual tax ranges from $1.00 in Arkansas to $2.00 in Mississippi), it has unquestionably been a deterrent to voting in the five southern states. Other requirements related to the poll tax may also tend to discourage voting. For example, in Mississippi the voter must present not only his current poll tax receipt but also proof that he has paid poll taxes for the two preceding years, and in Virginia a new voter must pay poll taxes for the previous three years unless he has just moved into the state or has just reached voting age. Thus the obligation to pay the tax must be met consistently for a voter to retain his voting eligibility. Another requirement which seems to present a hardship for some voters is the regulation that one must present the poll tax receipt at the polls; a seemingly reasonable requirement from the standpoint of efficient registration administration, but one that penalizes a good many voters who lose or misplace their poll tax receipts.

Not all voters in these five states are subject to the poll tax; in Alabama, Arkansas and Virginia members of the armed forces are exempt, and in Mississippi and Texas the blind or maimed voter is not required to pay. The other specific provisions for each state are given in Chart II in the appendix.

PROPERTY OWNERSHIP: For many years, the ownership of property was a necessary requirement for voting in most elections, but today such a qualification is only rarely found in election codes. *The Book of States*[1] lists six states (Michigan, Montana, Nevada, New Mexico, Texas and Utah) which require proof of property ownership as a requisite to voting on bond issues and special assessments. In addition to these, Oklahoma requires property tax payment for voting on certain local bond issues; Rhode Island requires that a voter prove that he paid his taxes at least nine days before an election in order to vote on proposals to impose a tax or expend money in a town; and Vermont requires that most voters (with some exceptions) must present their tax receipt in order to participate in a town meeting. Where such requirements are still in effect, the intent is obviously to preclude irresponsible voting on financial decisions which may materially affect the tax rates of a community. The importance of property qualifications in our early history and their virtual elimination at the present time provide a significant indication of the progress of the American people toward eliminating class bias in voting provisions.

State Provisions for Voter Disqualification

The caliber of an electorate is determined not only by the provisions which qualify voters, but also by the provisions for culling undesirables from the citizenry and explicitly barring them from participation in elections. Three groups, paupers, insane and criminals, are regarded as unworthy and are, in most states, specifically prohibited from registering as voters.

PAUPERS: At least 11 states (Delaware, Louisiana,

---

[1] Chicago: Council of State Governments, 1958 (Vol. XII), pp. 20-21.

Maine, Massachusetts, Missouri, New Hampshire, Oklahoma, South Carolina, Texas, Virginia, and West Virginia) specifically disqualify "paupers" as voting registrants, but the term is variously defined in different states. Usually the inhabitants of poorhouses or other institutions where the impecunious are housed at public expense are not allowed to vote; but they do not lose their residence by virtue of living in such an institution, and when they leave the poorhouse and become self-supporting, they usually are able to qualify again as electors. There are special provisions in Louisiana, Massachusetts, Missouri, New Hampshire, and Oklahoma which extend the franchise to honorably discharged veterans even though they may live in a publicly-supported soldiers' or sailors' home. The rationale for disfranchising the indigent is obviously the converse of that which requires property ownership.

INSANITY: In all states the right to register is denied to the mentally unsound either by specific law or by judicial decision. All states except Alaska, Illinois, Indiana, Maine, Massachusetts, Michigan, Nebraska, New Hampshire, Ohio, Pennsylvania, Rhode Island, Tennessee, and Vermont have specific laws which prohibit idiots, lunatics, the insane, or persons *non compos mentis* (or all of these) from qualifying as electors; in the other states the courts have usually held that such persons may not vote. And in 14 states,[1] individuals who are "under guardianship" are disqualified. This term is usually applied to people who are legally under the supervision and control of a person or agency designated by the Court. In most states, the registrar is responsible for identifying and denying registration to all of the persons described in this section.

CRIMINALS: In every state, anyone who is confined to prison is ineligible to vote, and cannot usually regain his franchise without obtaining an official pardon which specifically restores civil rights. In some states, such as Illinois, Kentucky, Montana, New York and Oregon, the governor

---

[1] Arizona, Colorado, Delaware, Idaho, Kansas, Maine, Massachusetts, Minnesota, North Dakota, Ohio, Rhode Island, South Dakota, Wisconsin, and Wyoming.

has the power to restore a former convict to full civil rights; in other states, such as Connecticut and North Dakota, a special commission possesses the right; and in Rhode Island an act of the general assembly is required to restore voting rights. In Mississippi and Virginia, a person convicted by the state courts of one of the crimes which disfranchise must obtain a pardon from the governor or have his franchise rights restored by an act of the state legislature, but in Colorado the constitution provides that a formerly qualified voter who has served his prison term or is released by virtue of a pardon "shall without further action, be invested with all rights of citizenship."

Usually conviction for any infamous crime, felony or treason brings disfranchisement. Many state codes spell out specific crimes which will disfranchise—and a sordid list it is—including mainly serious violations such as sex offenses, use of a deadly weapon, bribery, burglary, and forgery. The loss of voting rights is also a common penalty for the violation of election laws by either the elector or the election official. In most states, any elector who bets on the outcome of an election, or attempts to bribe an election official, or attempts to—or does—sell his vote or purchase someone else's vote, or tries to intimidate voters is liable to disfranchisement, perhaps for his lifetime. Some of the regulations designed to prevent these infractions are discussed in detail in Chapter 3.

Concluding Comments

As we have seen, the laws which provide, protect and deny the right to vote are far from uniform for the 50 states, but they all fit within the general constitutional pattern. The questions which arise as one examines the regulations concern the effect of this legislation on both the quality and size of the electorate. Are some statutes unduly restrictive? Do they discourage the average elector from "bothering" to vote? Do all requirements fall equally and fairly on all potential electors? These and other questions may suggest lines for improvement and revision of the laws controlling the right to vote in the United States.

Chapter 2

THE REGISTRATION PROCESS

Why Registration Is Necessary

It is essential in a democratic system that public opinion be as accurately expressed as possible, and one means for such expression is the ballot. In order to afford the franchise to those who are "qualified" and to prevent the voting of anyone who either is not qualified or who attempts to cast more than one ballot—it being a basic democratic premise that each citizen should have only one vote—registration systems have been devised. When towns were small and neighbors knew one another, it was hardly necessary for the registrar of elections to have an official means of checking voters whom he knew personally. Increasing size of the electorate and increasing urbanization inevitably resulted in a loss of neighborly knowledge of one's fellow citizens, however, and the need for some means of identifying voters was recognized as early as 1800 when the Massachusetts legislature, soon followed by other New England states, enacted a registration law. In other sections of the country, registration systems were not established until after the Civil War, but by about 1890 most states had some arrangements for the systematic listing of voters, especially for the electorates in the cities.[1] For some time physical descriptions of voters were included in registration records for identification purposes, but since

[1] Joseph P. Harris, **Election Administration in the United States** (Washington: Brookings Institution, 1934), p. 18.

the 1920's the main test used for identification is the voter's signature. Today the registration of electors, although not universal, is common practice in all but a few sparsely-populated rural areas in the United States. Such a system provides a check-list, and no one whose name does not appear on the list (where registration is required) may vote. If the list shows that an individual has already voted, he cannot cast another ballot, nor can any other person cast a ballot in his stead.

Kinds of Registration Systems

Several general classifications may be applied to registration systems: periodic or permanent depending on whether the elector must re-register at stated intervals or not, and personal or non-personal depending on whether the elector may only register in person or whether the laws also provide for his registration by mail.

PERIODIC AND PERMANENT REGISTRATION: Periodic registration has gradually been replaced by permanent systems in many states, but 14 still retain some form of periodic registration for certain areas. In New York, for example, voters in certain towns must register annually in order to retain their standing as qualified electors; in Wyoming, electors must register before every general election; in Iowa, Louisiana and Missouri, voters in specified areas must register every four years, in Nebraska every six years and in South Carolina all voters must re-register every ten years.

Since 1923, when Minnesota first enacted a permanent registration law, 34 states have instituted statewide permanent registration. Only Arkansas and Texas have no formal registration systems of any kind. The description of specific registration requirements for each state (found in Chart III in the appendix) shows clearly which states have permanent registration, but the common element in all of them is that the elector registers only once and so long as he continues to vote with a certain regularity, does not change his residence, his name or his party affiliation, and does not become disqualified for other reasons, he need not re-register.

There are disadvantages to a periodic system of registration from the standpoint of both the voter and the registrar. For the voter, the necessity of re-registering is a nuisance; it requires time and attention to meet the deadline. And in some areas where registration offices are open only a few days per month or only sporadically throughout the year, and where there is no provision for absentee registration, the voter who is traveling or who is ill may find it not only inconvenient but even impossible to register at the proper time. For the registrar, re-doing a registration list every few years involves more clerical and administrative work and expense than the continuous revision of lists under a permanent system. On the other hand, some analysts of electoral procedure maintain that a periodic system is the only sure way of obtaining a "clean list", that is, an accurate list of all voters who are currently in good standing, since under a permanent system, the name of a voter who has moved from a district or is otherwise disqualified may not be removed from the lists for several years. In spite of such criticisms, the permanent system has grown in favor and actual use. Most experts commend the efficiency, economy and general accuracy of a permanent registration system, and it is further suggested that the convenience for the voter is an encouragement to his voting—a not unimportant consideration in the light of the poor participation record of the American electorate. Furthermore, a centralized system of permanent registration, organized and run by a professional staff, is likely to be more accurate and free from fraud than a decentralized system under which precinct officers, temporarily appointed for the job at the recommendation of their political parties, undertake to register voters at frequent intervals.

PERSONAL REGISTRATION: Whether the system is periodic or permanent, the predominance of personal registration provisions in most states suggests the desirability of having the voter appear in person at the registrar's office. Even where arrangements are provided for registering by mail, the civilian voter must always have the affidavit of registration notarized except when special arrangements are made for the physically incapacitated voter. The advantages of having a voter present himself are obvious: personal information on age, residence, occupation and so forth can be more accurately elicited and recorded, any question about qualifications can be cleared up immediately, and the voter himself can be more thoroughly instructed concerning the regulations pertaining to his suffrage.

ABSENTEE REGISTRATION: Since many voters may find it impossible to register in person for a variety of reasons such as business obligations, enrollment in an academic institution, military service, or ill health, 21 states[1] provide for absentee or non-personal registration for certain civilians. The specific provisions are found in the state summaries of registration in the appendix.

The Administration of a Registration System

REGISTRATION OFFICIALS: The state official who ordinarily assumes legal responsibility for the entire election system is the Secretary of State. Any question regarding election privileges or requirements may be directed to him or to the official registrar in a voter's local district. The Secretary usually has a multi-membered Election Board or Commission to assist him in formulating policy and supervising election practice. In the county, the registration official may be known by a variety of titles: Recorder, Clerk, Auditor or Registrar. Or the authority for county registration may be vested in a board such as the Board of Election Supervisors, the County Board of Registrars, the County Election Commission or the Board of Civil Authority. Locally the registrar may be the municipal or town clerk or a justice of the peace. In short, there is no

---

[1] Arizona, California, Colorado, Hawaii, Idaho, Indiana, Iowa, Kansas, Michigan, Minnesota, Montana, New Mexico, New York, North Carolina, Ohio, Oregon, Rhode Island (for "shut-in" voters only), Tennessee, West Virginia, Wisconsin, Wyoming.

uniformity of title or structure in the administration of the various state systems. Usually local election officers are appointed, while the county and state board members are often elected for a term of several years. Most election boards and commissions are carefully balanced with representatives from both major parties.

The local registrar is entrusted with administering and executing the multifarious details of the registration system. His work is largely clerical, for in addition to maintaining registration lists, he keeps records on personnel, voting statistics, financial accounts, and cases of election irregularities with which the election board may deal. The registrar is also responsible for ascertaining whether a particular elector fulfills the necessary qualifications. In states where the registrars administer a literacy test and determine whether an applicant has correctly "interpreted" or "understood" a section of the state constitution, the registrar has, as we have noted in discussing electoral requirements, wide latitude for individual judgment and discretion. He is also legally empowered to administer oaths and issue affidavits attesting to the accuracy and legality of an elector's claims about his qualifications.

REVISION OF THE REGISTRATION LISTS: In most states it is also the registrar's duty to revise the registration lists; thus he has power to cancel registrations as well as make them. With the mobility of the American population and the precise residence requirements imposed by the states, this job of keeping the voting lists in good order requires constant attention. There are several methods by which information on voters is gathered by registration boards.

In some states, the registrar is empowered to make regular house-to-house canvasses; in others, he canvasses by mail. Kentucky provides for a house-to-house survey to be undertaken in first-class cities at least 30 days before any election by two investigators appointed by the Board of Registration. Such a canvass may be requested for specific precincts by the parties. In Maryland, a canvass may be undertaken by the judges of election early in January of every even-numbered year. In different-sized cities and population groups in Missouri, various provisions are made for canvasses to be conducted by mail or in person five weeks before elections. In Illinois the County Clerk is authorized to conduct periodic canvasses of his registration lists, and in Ohio the Board of Elections is empowered to conduct an annual check on registration. The County Clerk in Illinois mails a certificate of registration to each registered voter in counties under 500,000 every two or four years. If the certificate is returned unopened by the post office, the elector is then notified to come to the clerk's office within a week or ten days to "prove" his residence. Thus the burden of proof is shifted to the voter to prove the validity of his residence and his registration. West Virginia provides for a biennial check of the registration list if the County Court deems such a check necessary. In South Carolina, the boards of registration meet 30 days before any election and delete from the registration list the name of any voter who has become disqualified, has changed his residence, or has died. Voters whose names are cancelled are notified by registered mail at the address shown on the registration lists. If a voter's name has been unfairly or incorrectly removed from the lists, he is entitled to a hearing if he answers the notice from the registration board. In Louisiana, too, an annual canvass is made by the registrar, who then notifies by mail any elector whose registration is questioned. If the elector does not appear in answer to the notification, his name is finally cancelled from the register.

Another method of gleaning information relevant to the purgation of registration lists is to require reports from various state departments, health authorities, utility companies, and from the courts. In Ohio, required monthly reports from the county health officer, probate judge and the clerk of the court of common pleas enable the Board of Elections to remove from the registration files names of electors who have died or who have been committed to asylums or to prison. In Illinois, the County Clerk may use information from utility companies, the post office or other sources to determine when voters move from one residence to another, and the statutes give him the initiative in notifying electors of the procedure for transferring the registration. In Kentucky, every supplier of gas, water, phone service and electricity operating in each county is required by law to report to the County Clerk on the fifth business day of every month the names of all persons who have moved in or out of the county, and every city department is required to notify the Board weekly of anyone who has moved. The Clerk may, on the basis of reliable information, transfer the registration records from one precinct to another or otherwise change the registration, but he is required to notify the voter that he has revised the record. The Clerk is also empowered to clear the registration lists of the names of all those who have been committed for insanity or crime or who have moved away. Maryland also provides for official notice from the appropriate agencies of all electors who are deceased, or who have been convicted or institutionalized. In Michigan, the Clerk is required to check with the register of vital statistics at least once a month and is empowered to cancel all registrations of electors who have died.

Other excellent sources of information are the annual surveys conducted in various states. In Maine the assessors conduct an annual check each spring, visiting every building in every town and city, and listing all owners and occupants with information on age, name, and occupation; this compilation provides invaluable information for revision of registration lists. A similar procedure is followed in Massachusetts where an annual register of all persons is compiled by the police. If a voter is not included in this register, he is notified in June, and if he can present adequate evidence of his right to be reinstated on the registration list, his name is added.

One of the best "clues" to a voter's continued existence as registered is his voting record. A number of states have therefore set up definite time intervals for eliminating non-voters from registration lists. In such states the registration officers check the records after each election and cancel registrants who have not voted within recent years; such action is not necessary, of course, in a periodic system, but it is extremely important in a permanent one. The following summary (although the survey of election data on which it is based was not exhaustive) will give an indication of the time spans established by different states:

> REGISTRATION CANCELLED AFTER TWO YEARS OF NON-VOTING: Arizona; California; Colorado; Florida; Hawaii; Indiana; Kansas; Kentucky; Louisiana, in parishes with cities over 300,000; Minnesota, in cities of first class over 90,000 and less than 200,000; Missouri, in some areas; Montana; Nevada; Ohio; Oregon; Pennsylvania; Rhode Island (26 months ending with December 31); Wisconsin; and Wyoming.

> REGISTRATION CANCELLED AFTER FOUR YEARS OF NON-VOTING: Delaware; Illinois; Iowa; Louisiana, in areas other than those cited above; Minnesota, in areas other than those cited above; Missouri, in some areas; Nebraska, in cities of 7,000 to 40,000; New Jersey; New Mexico; New York; Oklahoma; Tennessee; Washington; and West Virginia.

> REGISTRATION CANCELLED AFTER FIVE YEARS OF NON-VOTING: Georgia and Maryland.

> REGISTRATION CANCELLED AFTER SIX YEARS OF NON-VOTING: North Carolina.

TIMES FOR REGISTRATION OF VOTERS: The official registration periods, that is the days and hours when the voter may register, are different for every state. In a large number of states, registration closes several weeks before each election to enable the registrars to compile final lists of voters and to distribute official lists to party and poll officials. The registrars are required by law to announce the times for registration in local newspapers and in official notices for wide publicity is important to ensure that no elector is prevented from registering because of uncertainty or ignorance about the proper time for registration.

In most permanent systems of registration, the office of the registrar is open during regular business hours throughout the year except for the period immediately preceding the election; in other states with periodic registration, the registrar's office is open only on stated days. The states which have permanent and periodic registration are listed below; and the voter is advised to check registration hours with his local registration board.

PERMANENT REGISTRATION: Alabama, Alaska, Arizona, California, Colorado, Connecticut, Delaware, Florida, Georgia, Hawaii, Idaho, Illinois, Indiana, Kentucky, Maine, Massachusetts, Michigan, Mississippi, Montana, Nevada, New Hampshire, New Jersey, New Mexico, North Carolina, Oklahoma, Oregon, Pennsylvania, Rhode Island, South Dakota, Tennessee, Utah, Vermont, Washington, and West Virginia.

PERMANENT REGISTRATION IN SOME AREAS: Iowa, Kansas, Louisiana, Maryland, Minnesota, Missouri, Nebraska, New York, North Dakota, Ohio, Virginia, Wisconsin.

PERIODIC REGISTRATION IN ALL AREAS: South Carolina (every 10 years); Wyoming (every general election).

LATE REGISTRATION: Registration laws are somewhat more flexible than the precise description of hours and days for regular registration would suggest. Many states take special account of the voter who has been ill, or who qualifies to register (by becoming 21, or fulfilling the residence requirement, or returning from military service) after the official registration deadline. Reference to the provisions for each state in Chart III will reveal the many exceptions to the regular registration procedure. The interpretation of most registration rules is decidedly in the voter's favor, even to the point of allowing some voters to produce evidence of their qualifications at the polls and to be duly registered on election day.

WHAT THE VOTER MUST DO TO REGISTER: The registration procedure is in most states quite simple, and although variations exist from state to state, it is possible to describe the usual steps. When an elector goes to the office of the registrar, he is asked to answer under oath certain questions about his residence, age, citizenship, and all of the other qualifications. Since these are the data by which the voter will thereafter be identified at the polls, he must be very careful to answer correctly and to sign his name as he ordinarily does. In most states, the full name is required, or at least the middle initial if the middle name is not used. Since the signature is the key to the identification of the voter, it is very important that he sign in his usual manner—often a signature is disallowed on a nominating petition or in signing at the polls because it does not compare exactly with the original signature on the registration record. If an elector is a naturalized citizen, he should take with him the *official papers* (original or certified copy) which attest to his naturalization; photographic copies of such papers are not suitable. If the registrant does not have official papers, he should write the Immigration and Naturalization Service; in some cases, they will furnish this information directly to the registration officials if the registrant so requests.

The registrant must also be prepared to meet the literacy, poll tax and other special requirements for registration in his state. The specific provisions for literacy are given in Chart I in the appendix; the voter should note that most states make arrangements for excusing or specially testing registrants who are physically disabled or who are blind. There are also certain voters who are exempt from the imposition of the poll tax. (See Chart II.)

In 14 states, the registrant receives a certificate of registration (Alabama, Florida, Illinois, Indiana, Iowa, Louisiana, Maryland, New Mexico, Oklahoma, Pennsylvania, South Carolina, Tennessee, West Virginia, Wisconsin), and in a number of them presentation of this certificate is also a requisite of voting.

THE CHALLENGE OF REGISTRANTS: Just as there are party representatives whose job it is to challenge voters at the polls, so party challengers are usually present at any public registration or revision session for the purpose of questioning registration applicants. Grounds for such challenge are clearly stated in the laws—usually insufficient residence or failure to meet other required qualifications. The challenge is declared to the official board or registrar as a person applies to register, or a challenge may have been filed in writing in advance of the public session. The registering authority acknowledges the challenge, questions the applicant under oath as to his retort to the challenge, and then passes on the validity of the application or the challenge. The voter who is refused the right to register is afforded recourse to a higher election authority, or, failing of success within the administrative branch, may take his final appeal to the courts. Such a challenge may be only a party maneuver to harrass registrants of the opposition party, but more often it serves constructively as a check on attempts by the unqualified to gain access to the ballot.

TRANSFER OF REGISTRATION: The elector is obliged, under most state requirements, to notify the registrar when he changes his residence, his name or his party affiliation. In some states, a voter is required to re-register under these circumstances, but in most states, notification of the appropriate officials suffices. The state-by-state summaries of transfer provisions are given in Chart III in the appendix, but a few general comments may be made. Whenever an elector moves from one precinct to another or from county to county within a state, he is usually required to notify the registration authorities of his new address and to request the cancellation of his previous registration. If he moves during the time when registration is closed, he is, in certain states, permitted to vote in his former precinct for one election immediately following the change of residence, but he is expected to change his registration as soon as possible. In some cases, however, the elector may not vote in his old precinct and may not

35

register in his new district until he has lived there for the legally prescribed length of time.

The elector whose name is changed either through marriage or through a court order is usually directed to notify the registration officials so that they may revise their records. In some states a new registration is required; in others the voter may simply notify the authorities in person or by mail of his change of name, and his registration card will be corrected without complete re-registration. And in certain instances, especially in the case of a woman who has married, the name change may be effected when she goes to the polls on election day.

In all but two or three of the fifty states, an elector must be enrolled as a member of a political party before he may participate in the primary by which party candidates are nominated. Enrollment in an American political party does not entail an official act of joining the party, payment of dues or, in fact, even active participation in party activities; enrollment is usually achieved by the simple declaration by the voter when he registers that he is a member of a certain party. In some states, if a voter's affiliation is challenged at the polls by members of the party with which he claims affiliation, he must swear under oath that he has supported the nominees of that party in previous elections or that he intends to support them in the next general election. In other words, party affiliation in the United States is a matter of voter intention rather than an officially-executed membership. In nearly every state, an elector is prevented by law from transferring from one party to another within at least one month and usually for several months before the forthcoming primary. The purpose of such a regulation is to prevent members of one party from temporarily shifting their affiliation in order to participate in the opposition party's nominations. This practice, known as "raiding", is a means by which members of one party might participate in the primary of their opponents in order to swell the vote for the weakest opposition candidate; if the "raid" is successful, competition is reduced for the raiders' own candidate in the general election. The elaborate arrangements in most states for changing party affiliation and the time restrictions on voting after an affiliation change strongly deter most voters from attempting a shift for other than honest purposes—that is, a change of party loyalty made in good faith.

Concluding Comments

Registration laws, like all other legislation dealing with the voting process, are characterized by the widest imaginable diversity. In spite of strong and persistent pressure from civic groups concerned with the honesty and efficiency of elections, many states still have inadequate systems for keeping track of their voters. Unquestionably the Model Registration System[1] advocated by the National Municipal League has had an important influence on the revision of various state systems, but a cursory look at the multiplicity of state provisions in Chart III is enough to suggest that the job of providing an equitable and consistent registration system within each state and for each state is far from finished. The purpose of such a system, succinctly declared in the Tennessee Election Code[2], "to secure the freedom and purity of the ballot box . . . by preventing plural voting and by requiring voters to vote in election precincts where they reside," has not yet been fully realized throughout the country.

---

[1] Model Voter Registration System (New York: National Municipal League, Partial Revision, 1957).
[2] Section 2-301.

Chapter 3

THE VOTING PROCESS

The average voter, were he to look at the election code which controls his voting privilege, would undoubtedly be overwhelmed by the myriad regulations dealing with every facet of the election process. A number of the codes run to two or three hundred pages and detail precisely the election personnel, their duties, and the exact procedures which they and the voters must follow if an election is to be "legal". Statutory laws which set forth the framework, and in many cases the minutiae, of election administration comprise an integral part of the electoral system of the United States; therefore, it seems appropriate to discuss the election officials and their role in the voting process before examining the requirements for the voter.

Election Administration

The administration of elections, as stated earlier, falls mainly within the governmental jurisdiction of each state, and is more specifically the responsibility of the Secretary of State or a state official of similar rank. The power is delegated by his office to election boards or their counterparts at the county level, and then to the countless ward and precinct officials or election judges who conduct the actual polling in the neighborhoods. Many procedures connected with the polling are regularized throughout the state: registration requirements, polling hours and the methods for casting and tallying ballots are usually standard. Other decisions such as the rearrangement of election districts to accommodate population changes, whether to use paper ballots or voting machines, and the arrangements for election supplies and polling locations are within the province of local officials, and are more likely to vary from place to place within a state.

Each polling place is run by at least two election judges or supervisors who belong to different political parties—in all states where there are two viable parties to provide such representatives. In some states the law requires that these judges be of "upright character", (in all other states, naturally, this is assumed!) and usually the judges are also required to take an oath that they will properly and honestly perform their duties. For obvious reasons, such judges may not themselves be candidates for office, nor may they be actively engaged in any candidate's campaign. In sizable polling districts with large numbers of voters, several clerks may be appointed, again on a bipartisan basis, to assist the judges with the various jobs of verifying and checking off the voter's name in the registration book, giving him a ballot, making certain that he understands the procedure for marking a ballot or using a voting machine, assisting the physically disabled or blind voter, and counting and reporting the final results after the polls close.

In some states, notably Connecticut, Georgia, Michigan, Oklahoma and South Dakota, the state election boards conduct training schools and seminars for local election officials. The Michigan Director of Elections, who serves under the Secretary of State, arranges for such training sessions for county clerks or their representatives before every primary and biennial general election. South Dakota holds similar sessions, but less frequently. In Georgia, the State Registration and Election Information Board prepares and distributes election information to the local registrars and also conducts seminars and meetings for the instruction of local election officers. In Connecticut, town clerks and registrars attend two state-wide meetings during the year for the purpose of discussing election laws and procedures, and in Oklahoma, the Secretaries of the county election boards attend election law study conferences conducted under the auspices of the State Election Board. Such efforts to train polling officials, in a sense to educate them toward professionalization, and also to solicit their views on possible improvements in electoral legislation and procedure represent a long step ahead on the road toward unimpeachable election administration.

In addition to the *official* poll workers, that is those paid by the state or locality, every voting place usually has severtal poll watchers, challengers and party checkers in attendance. State laws provide for their appointment and duties, but these people cannot be considered "official" and are not entitled to count ballots or participate in the other official business of the polls. The watchers and challengers are at the polls to serve their political parties rather than the state; their job is to defend party interests by challenging any voter whom they believe to be legally unqualified, and by questioning any election practice prejudicial to their party's interests. Several such representatives may serve at each poll, and they are entitled to witness all election transactions throughout the day until all ballots have been counted and recorded. Of course, they may not interfere with any individual in the exercise of his franchise, and they are specifically prohibited from any type of electioneering. They are mainly watchdogs, alert to any threat to partisan interests; and their partisan alertness is inevitably valuable to the public interest for, like the dog watching the cat watch the mouse, the poll watchers watch each other. Party checkers may also be at the polls to keep a running count on party members as they vote. If, toward the end of the polling hours, the list shows that known party supporters have not voted, they are rounded up by partisan workers and urged to go to the polls.

The Polling Process

CHALLENGE OF VOTERS: Generally the laws describe the exact procedure for the challenge of voters, from the grounds on which a challenge may be brought to the specific questions which the voter must answer if he is to refute the challenge. Challengers may question an individual's right to vote on a number of counts — betting on the election results, attempting to vote a second time (or "repeating"), or simply voting under an improper registration. When a voter is challenged for these or other reasons, the decision on the validity of the challenge is made by the presiding election judges. In Missouri, for example, when a voter is challenged, he is placed under oath by the election judges and questioned by them and by the challenger. If a majority of the judges find him qualified, the elector may vote, but if he is found not qualified, he may even be arrested for impersonating a voter. In Oregon and several other states, any election board clerk has the right to challenge a voter whom he suspects to be unqualified. The challenged voter can vote if he declares under oath that he is qualified, but in such a case, the poll book contains the notation "challenged and sworn" and the ballot is specially marked so that it can be discounted if the challenge is finally upheld.

Usually there is not adequate time during polling hours to allow for the appeal and reinstatement of a challenged voter, so if some means is not provided for allowing such a person to vote provisionally, he may unjustifiably lose his vote. For this reason, most states arrange for challenges to be made before election day. Complete registration lists including both regular and absentee voters are ordinarily sent by the election boards to the political parties and candidates before each election. If a party challenges a name on this official list, the challenge may be heard and judged by the election board several weeks before the election. The elector then has adequate time to appeal to the county registrar, the county court or another legally-designated appeal board for a reversal of an adverse decision. In New Mexico, for example, the county chairman of each political party receives advance lists of the registered voters, and during the 45 days before an election he may petition for the instatement of a member of his party or may challenge the registration of members of the opposition. Similarly in Maryland, official registration lists

41

are publicly posted and are also distributed to candidates and political parties at least 29 days before the general election. Any person may file his objection to another registered voter with the Board of Supervisors, so long as he files his complaint several days before the election. Two members of the Board of Supervisors sit to hear objections and are authorized to decide all cases immediately after hearing them; but the challenged voter may appeal from their decision to the county or city courts. The Massachusetts law provides that in a city, a challenge must be filed at least 14 days before an election and in a town a challenge must be entered at least four days ahead. After investigating the challenge, the registrar hears the case of the challenged voter and then decides whether his name shall be retained or struck from the register. In Hawaii, a challenge, elaborating in writing the specific grounds for the question, is sent to the election clerk; he then notifies the party of the challenged voter so that a defense can be arranged. In Maine, the voter is allowed to defend himself; the law requires that a challenged voter must be notified at least six hours before the close of the final registration session so that he may appear before the registration board and defend his right to vote.

This random sample of various challenge and appeal procedures includes most of the checks employed. While the challenge is still an important safeguard against fraudulent registration and voting, it is of less consequence now that registration systems have been formalized and improved.

POLLING PLACE: Local election officials entrusted with the choice of locations for polling places usually select a school or other public building which is convenient for the voters. The major restriction, common to all states, is that polls not be located in a place where alcoholic beverages are sold, or in a location which is not easily accessible to all electors. Election day regulations prohibit crowds from milling around the polls, and prohibit loitering within a certain distance (usually one hundred feet) of the polling place. Further attempts to insulate electors from any pressure or intimidation extends to the prohibition of the distribution of campaign literature within a prescribed distance of the polls.

In order to maintain the decorum of the polling place, election officials are usually authorized as temporary sheriffs with the right to imprison any troublemaker (after he has voted) for a period of 24 hours; this temporarily-assumed police power is often reinforced by the presence of the local sheriff or a policeman assigned to the poll. Rarely do officials exercise these powers, but their possession of them is further assurance that the balloting will be orderly and uninterrupted.

Polling hours differ from state to state and Chart IV in the appendix gives the specific times for each state. Most election codes provide that each citizen is entitled to released time from his employment for the purpose of voting; in a few states, the voter is legally allowed up to four hours off from his employment with no deduction in pay or other penalty for the time missed, but the more usual provision allows two or three hours. Any employer who does not honor this time-off provision (provided the employee has made arrangements prior to election day) is liable to fine or imprisonment.

The special importance of the voter on election day in a democracy is suggested by other provisions. In most states, an elector on his way to the polls is immune from arrest except for breach of the peace or treason or felony. Voters are also exempt from military duty on election day except in time of war or in case of public emergency.

POLLING PROCEDURE: Every effort is made at the polls to achieve an orderly and efficient voting procedure: voters are required to take their turn in line, they are restricted to an area a certain distance from the actual balloting booths so that the voter in the booth enjoys privacy; they must follow the prescribed routine. The voter gives his name to the election clerk, who says the name clearly and distinctly for the benefit of the challengers or watchers, he presents any registration certificate or other identification or receipt which may be required by the particular laws of the state, he signs the registration book or record, he casts his ballot in the prescribed manner, and he must leave the polls promptly after depositing the ballot in the appropriate box or pulling the lever on the voting machine. Various regulations common to most codes are intended to expedite balloting; for example, voters are usually legally limited to two or three minutes' time in the voting booth. If a voter spoils his first ballot, by marking it incorrectly, or spilling ink on it or otherwise defacing it, he is entitled without question in all states to a second ballot and in some states to a third. This provision, of course, applies only where paper ballots are used. Oregon in what appears to be a sensible precaution, further provides that if an elector spoils three ballots, it is concluded that he requires assistance and help is provided by two election board clerks!

In states where voting machines are used the procedure for voting varies somewhat. The procedures for identifying and challenging the elector are the same, but the voter, of course, never receives a ballot but simply steps into the curtained booth when his turn comes and votes by adjusting the levers on the machine. Since 1892 when voting machines were first used in Lockport, New York, many states have adopted laws enabling local election boards to provide machines, and their use is now widespread. Although difficulties have arisen when machines have broken down and no alternative means for voting was available, the efficiency and accuracy of machine tabulation of votes are highly advantageous, especially in areas where the vote is large.

THE ASSISTED VOTER: In the American election experience, it has been found that arrangements for assisting a voter must be strictly regulated, since in former years this practice was considered to be "one of the principal sources of election manipulation."[1] Thus several considerations are important in the provision of assistance to voters who are physically disabled, blind or illiterate. It

---

[1] Harris, Election Administration, p. 227.

is important first to establish who will qualify for help, that is, who should be assisted; then, to specify who is to give the help, an election official or a friend selected by the voter himself; and finally, to describe what kind of help may be given. The overall concern, of course, is that the voter's privacy of decision and secrecy of vote not be needlessly jeopardized because of his infirmity; or, to put it another way, that a voter's disability not place him in a situation where he is subject to coercion or pressure in deciding or casting his vote. Since no assisted voter can be entirely independent, the problem is intrinsically insoluble, but the legislation contains a variety of provisions to minimize the difficulty.

Who qualifies for assistance as a physically disabled elector? Some states deny help at the polls unless such disability was noted on the original registration. Other states, however, consider it sufficient if the voter's disability is "apparent" to the registrar. In some cases simply the elector's statement that he needs help suffices to obtain aid. Taking these variations into account, usually blindness, inability to use one's hands, or any other physical ailment which prevents an elector from reading or marking his ballot is considered disability warranting assistance. Certain states specifically, and all states implicitly, rule out intoxication as a justifiable reason for assistance; as the Illinois and Wisconsin statutes tersely state: "Intoxication shall not be regarded as a physical disability . . . ." In Maine a person may also request help in marking his ballot if his religious beliefs prevent him from doing so himself.

There is always a danger, of course, that the person who aids a voter may either unduly influence the vote or deliberately not mark the ballot as the voter directs. To prevent the possibility of such fraudulent attempts, many state laws provide that assistance to a voter may only be given by the officials at the polling place and further provide that a disabled voter shall be accompanied to the booth and assisted by not one but two election judges who must be of different political parties. In some states, Wisconsin for instance, the voter can select the officials whom he wants to help him. In contrast to the states which provide only for official help to the disabled voter is Nevada which provides that a disabled voter may be aided by any elector he may designate other than an election officer; the restriction here is that no person may assist more than one voter — a protection against a concerted attempt to influence the votes of a sizable number of dependent voters. This same type of restriction is imposed in states where the voter can choose whom he wants to assist him either from the election officials or the qualified voters. In Minnesota, for example, the voter may choose another qualified elector to help him, but that person must not assist more than three voters at one election. If a voter cannot understand English (in those states where fluency in English is not a requirement for voting), the election officials may select two persons to serve as interpreters, again so long as they are of two different political parties. In North Carolina at a general election, *any* voter is entitled to request help from a member of his family who may go with the voter into the booth and render such help as is needed; and in case of a physically disabled person, he may receive help from a relative or from a "marker" — one of a group of people recommended to the county board of election by their county party organization for their possession of good moral character and the "requisite educational qualifications". Almost without exception, a blind voter is free to choose a member of his family or another qualified elector from the election district to help him; usually the blind are not limited to help only from election officials.

. Laws vary also about the kinds of assistance which can be given a disabled, blind or illiterate voter. The common procedure. is for the judges to accompany the voter into the booth and mark the ballot as he directs them. In Maryland, however, it would seem that the protection of the voter's independence might prove a handicap to him, for there the voter must dictate his choices to the relative or election officials who help him. The law reads that no one is to read the ballot to him, but many ballots run to inordinate lengths and dictation of all the names from memory would be quite a feat. In Kentucky, too, meticulous care is taken to insure an illiterate voter's freedom from coercion and to afford him the right to mark his own ballot; there, the voter tells the clerk what his party and candidate choice is, and the clerk in the presence of judges, the sheriff, the challengers and the voter puts a pencil dot in the proper place. The voter then goes to the booth and marks his own ballot; here, secrecy of voting is sacrificed to guarantee that the choice is the voter's.

The provisions for the assistance of the blind, the physicially disabled or the illiterate voter are all intended to afford him as much independence and secrecy as is possible under the circumstances. The laws vary but the purpose is uniform: to protect the voter and his vote.

BALLOTS: Many states send sample ballots to electors several days before the election, thus enabling the voter to familiarize himself with the names and issues on the ballot and facilitating voting at the polls. Nothing prevents the voter from taking the sample ballot or any other memorandum into the booth with him, and this is often helpful when a number of offices and issues are to be decided.

The only common characteristic among the states in balloting is the use of the Australian ballot; that is, an official ballot which is printed at public expense and at the direction of public officials and which contains only the names of candidates who are nominated according to legally established procedures.[1] Although such ballots are now used exclusively, this has been a relatively recent development in American voting practice. The first such ballot was adopted for limited use in Kentucky in 1888, but not until the late 1920's did all states adopt an official written ballot for all elections. Written ballots were used widely prior to the twentieth century, but the ballots were usually furnished by the political parties and were seldom uniform. Uniformity from state to state still does not exist

---

[1] Harris, **Election Administration**, p. 154.

in regard to the size and color of the ballots or the arrangement of the offices and candidates on them. Some states list candidates for national and state offices on separate ballots; some use one long ballot which includes all national and state candidates. In some states, such as Minnesota and Vermont, ballots for different levels of government are printed on different-colored paper, and Vermont even provides appropriately matching boxes to receive these ballots. In Wyoming, Alabama, Massachusetts and South Dakota, different colors are used to distinguish the primary ballots of the two major parties.

Not only do the length and color of ballots differ, but the actual form and arrangement of the names on the ballots are seldom the same from one state to another. There are two commonly-used arrangements known as the office-type (or Massachusetts) and party-column (or Indiana) ballot. In the former, candidates' names are listed together under the office for which they are running, with a party designation beside each name; in the latter, the candidates of each party are listed in separate columns with the name of the office for which they are contending listed beside the name. The party-column ballot enables a voter to cast a straight party ticket very easily by marking a single "X" in the box or circle at the top of the column, thus automatically casting his vote for all of the candidates of that party. With the office-type ballot, however, the voter must mark his choice for each political office. Even on this type of ballot, the voter may vote only for the candidates of a single party if he so desires, but he must consciously choose each candidate rather than casting a blanket party vote. Because it prompts the voter to make conscious choices, the office-type ballot is generally regarded as superior to the party-column, even though it encourages (or at least does not discourage) cross-party voting which some students of American politics see as further weakening party discipline in the two major parties.

Precaution must be taken to ensure that the marked ballot the voter places in the ballot box is the ballot that he himself marked. A practice called "endless chain ballot" grew up in the early days of American elections. A corrupt politician would stand outside the polls and give an already marked ballot to a bribed voter who would take it into the polling place, substitute it for the fresh ballot he was given by the poll officials and bring the unmarked ballot out to the vote buyer who could repeat the process time and again. The first link in such a chain was the acquisition of an official but unmarked ballot at the beginning of the polling day. To combat this and other chicanery, most states take careful precautions to ensure that packages of ballots are sealed until they are delivered to the polling place, and in some cases the precinct official must personally procure the ballots from a central distribution point and take them to his poll. Another precaution used by a number of states is a numbering system for the ballots. When the voter enters the polls and signs the poll list, his name is registered beside a number which corresponds to the number on the stub of the ballot which is handed to him. After he has marked the ballot, the elector hands the folded ballot to the election official who rechecks the number against the poll list, then usually tears the numbered stub from the ballot and deposits it in a separate box. Such a procedure ensures that the voter has marked his own ballot, but does not threaten the secrecy of his ballot since the identifying number is removed with the stub. The use of voting machines clearly obviates the precautions necessary to protect the integrity of the paper ballot.

CORRUPT PRACTICES AND ELECTION CRIMES: State legislation describing violations of election laws and the penalties for such infractions is exceedingly comprehensive. Separate laws deal with election officials in the performance of their official duties, the voter as an individual citizen, the political parties and their activities, and the candidates in the conduct of their campaigns. It is not possible here to discuss the corrupt practices legislation in detail, but it is important to emphasize that an extensive system of legal restraints circumscribes the activities of all participants in the electoral process.

Specific crimes which bring disfranchisement are de-

49

scribed in grim detail in most state codes, but it is relevant here to discuss the more general types of election violations which are penalized. Probably the most universally condemned activity is betting or the placing of a wager on the outcome of an election; such activity is variously punished in different states, but it is uniformly prohibited. An equally serious election offense is bribery or the attempt to buy or influence an elector's vote or the offer to sell one's own vote; these are penalized by fine or imprisonment, or both, as well as by disfranchisement for from two years to a lifetime. Perjury, in connection with affidavits or the oaths which an elector takes attesting to the accuracy of his statements, is punishable by fine and imprisonment; and fraud in connection with registration or the casting of a ballot is also punishable. In Rhode Island, for example, a conviction for a fraudulent attempt to vote by an unqualified voter disfranchises that individual for the future. In Washington, anyone who attempts to vote more than once is guilty of a gross misdemeanor and may not vote for two years thereafter.

Not only is the voter liable to have his franchise removed for cause, but in most states, the public official who tampers with the electoral procedure may also be disfranchised. For instance, in California and in Virginia, any public official who helps in any way with the illegal casting of a vote shall "forever be disqualified from exercising the right of franchise . . . ."

Employers are prevented from attempting to coerce the political decisions of their employees. A New Jersey statute, for example, requires forfeiture of a corporation charter if a corporation official is found guilty of undue political pressure, and a similar penalty exists in Tennessee and other states. In Rhode Island, any attempt by an employer to intimidate employees in voting, if discovered, results in the loss of that employer's voting privileges.

PRIMARY ELECTIONS: A primary is a preliminary election in which party nominees vie for their party's nomination for the particular office in which they are interested. Primaries are used at all levels of government to nominate candidates. The times for the state primaries vary from March to September, and the voter should check in his community to ascertain when and where the primary will be held.

In nearly all states only enrolled party members may participate in the primaries, and this is understandable, for a primary is essentially a party matter. It is the device through which party members express their preferences among the candidates for the person whom they will support in the general election; and, therefore, the primary is usually closed to all but reliable party members who take seriously their party's eventual success in the final election. Most state requirements for changing party affiliation discourage temporary or irresponsible shifting from one party to another, and these provisions serve the best interests of the major parties. In voting in a primary, the voter declares his party affiliation, and then, according to the variation in state laws, he may be given only the ballot for that party, or he may be given a single ballot on which he can vote only for the candidates of a single party (Idaho, Minnesota and North Dakota) or he may be given several ballots from which he is to use one and discard the others (Michigan, Montana, Utah and Wisconsin), or as in the case of Washington which has an open primary, the voter may vote for people in different parties for different offices.

In a few states the primaries for the two parties are held in separate places. And in a few others, such as Rhode Island and Connecticut, Republican and Democratic primaries are held at different times, sometimes as much as a week apart.

Provisions are also made in some states for a second or run-off primary in case no candidate receives a majority of the votes cast in the first primary. The second primary is prevalent in the South where the winner of the Democratic nomination is almost bound to win the general election because he seldom has significant Republican competition. Florida law calls for a run-off to be held five weeks before the general elections, and Tennessee and Louisiana provide for such a primary to be set within three or four weeks after the first primary.

There are other nominating devices such as state and local nominating conventions, held either before the primary, or as in one or two states, after the primary. Since we are primarily concerned with the voting activities of the average voter, however, these devices are only of incidental interest because they are usually limited to a comparatively few party supporters rather than the elec- torate as a whole.

Concluding Comments

An honest and accurate polling process is a *sine qua non* of democracy. Even though an individual citizen may meet the requirements and be enrolled as a qualified voter, his status as an elector is meaningless unless he can be certain that his vote will be exactly counted. Ballots, just as appropriately as bank balances, require careful accounting. Although, as we have seen, the incidence of corruption and dishonesty is considerably lower today than it was in the early part of this century, there is still a wide margin for improvement. Use of voting machines has almost elim- inated tabulation errors in many elections, but there is still need for further simplification and regularization of polling throughout the county. All procedures pertaining to voting should be examined with an eye toward making the bal- loting results an absolutely accurate registration of public opinion on candidates and issues.

Chapter 4

ABSENTEE VOTING

Civilian Absentee Voting

Since the beginning of the twentieth century, Americans have been on the road, traveling extensively for every conceivable reason both serious and frivolous. Because on any election day, hundreds of thousands and possibly millions of voters are likely to be temporarily away from home, it has become essential to provide some means for them to participate in elections *in absentia*. The means, of course, is the absentee ballot. The first civilian absentee voting law providing that a qualified voter could, on the presentation of a certificate, vote at any polling place within the state was adopted in Vermont in 1896. Since that time all states have experimented with absentee voting systems, and today all except New Mexico, Pennsylvania, and South Carolina have laws enabling civilians either to cast their ballots in person before the election if they anticipate absence from the county or state on election day or to cast their ballots by mail.

The recommendation of most experts is that absentee voting privileges should not be limited to certain elections, and today 41 states provide for some form of absentee voting in all primary and general elections. Only Connecticut, Delaware, Massachusets, New Hampshire, New York, North Carolina and Rhode Island limit absentee voting to the general election alone.

The difficulties connected with an absentee voting system

are obvious. The danger of fraud, always a possibility in any election, increases when ballots are marked outside the carefully regularized procedure of the polling place. The provision of alternative arrangements also means more work for the election officials, for they must provide special absentee ballots, make them available well in advance of the election, arrange for their official distribution, establish a receiving agent for the marked ballots, distribute them to the proper polling place, verify their validity, and make certain that they are properly tabulated in the final count. Although a minor problem compared to the administrative headaches, it should also be noted that it is difficult to challenge an absentee voter. Usually absentee lists are posted before the election and challenge may be made prior to election day, but even so, the refutation of the challenge or provision for appeal from a challenge which is upheld is difficult when the voter is not present at the polls. These drawbacks are clearly outweighed, however, by the democratic imperative of enabling as many citizens as possible to participate in elections.

By describing in detail the electors who are eligible to vote by absentee ballot, many states forestall the possibility that voters will cast an absentee ballot simply for their own convenience. On the other hand, eligibility requirements should never be so complicated or overly restrictive that they preclude voting by a large number of people who rightfully deserve the privilege. There is obviously little virtue in providing absentee voting opportunities at all if excessively rigid or technical requirements discourage the majority of voters from even attempting to comply. The proper balance between voter convenience and honest elections is difficult to strike, but the best equilibrium point must be found if a system is to be acceptable.

ELIGIBILITY FOR CIVILIAN ABSENTEE VOTING: A large number of states have very broad eligibility provisions which, although phrased differently in different laws, essentially afford absentee voting privileges to anyone who is absent for any reason from his election district or state on election day.[1] Such flexible provisions accord with the recommendations of most students of the election process who maintain that the reason for a voter's absence is immaterial since the purpose of the absentee vote is simply to meet the needs of the voter, not to favor one group of electors over another. However, some states do limit absentee voting rights to electors who are absent in the conduct of business or because of professional or educational commitments. With few exceptions, states also provide for absentee voting by voters who are unable to appear at the polls in person because they are ill, or infirm, or physically disabled, but usually such an elector must submit a physician's certificate or a statement by a practitioner of Christian Science which attests to the legitimacy of the claimed physical disability or sickness. Certain states (Arizona, California, Colorado, Florida, Maine, Michigan, Minnesota, Vermont, Washington, and Wisconsin) also grant absent voting rights to electors who cannot personally go to the polls on election day because of the tenets of their religion, or because it is necessary for them to attend religious services or to maintain religious observances on the day of an election. The laws in Arkansas, Indiana, Michigan, New York, and Tennessee single out certain other groups of electors who specially deserve absentee voting rights: students, teachers, employees of railroads, traveling salesmen, legislators, actors and others. These groups are all presumably included in the more general provisions of the remainder of the states.

PROCEDURE FOR ABSENTEE BALLOTING: The general procedure for obtaining and marking an absentee ballot is essentially the same for all states, but the specific details of time of application, the election officers to whom the voter applies and the date for the return of the ballot

---

[1] Alaska, Arizona, California, Colorado, Connecticut, Florida, Georgia, Hawaii, Idaho, Kansas, Maryland, Massachusetts, Minnesota, Missouri, Montana, Nebraska, Nevada, New Hampshire, North Carolina, North Dakota, Ohio, Oregon, Pennsylvania, Rhode Island, South Dakota, Tennessee, Utah, Vermont, Virginia, Washington, West Virginia, Wisconsin, Wyoming.

are peculiar to each state. A state-by-state description of eligibility and absentee voting provisions is given in Chart V in the appendix. Safeguards against dishonest voting must be incorporated into any absentee voting system; provisions must be carefully drawn so that only qualified voters may obtain absentee ballots and so that the ballots will be marked accurately, honestly and without collusion. To meet the first requirement, all absentee voting systems require the elector or his agent to apply directly to an election official to obtain a ballot; the official checks the voter's record in the official files and furnishes a ballot only if the elector is found to be fully qualified. Many states compound the precaution by requiring that the voter's application be made on an official form obtainable only from the election board. In other states, a simple letter, postcard or even telephone call is acceptable for application. Usually the application for a ballot contains an affidavit form which must be completed and sworn to by the applicant in the presence of a notary public or other officer legally authorized to administer oaths. If a state requires such an affidavit in the case of military personnel, a commissioned officer or a non-commissioned officer of the rank of sergeant or petty officer is in most states regarded as legally competent to administer the oath on the affidavit; however, the affidavit requirement is sometimes waived altogether for servicemen. The affidavit declares that the information on the application concerning the voter's permanent voting residence, his qualifications to vote by absentee ballot and his biographical data are accurate.

Once the application and, where required, its notarized affidavit are received by the appropriate election officer, he checks the voter's name against the permanent registration records. If the registration is in good standing, and if the applicant's signature compares accurately with the signature in the registration files, the election officer will at the appropriate time before the elections (and the time varies considerably from state to state) send the voter all of the necessary ballots along with instructions for marking and returning them. The voter will receive

56

the ballots enclosed in an official envelope, sometimes called a voucher envelope, and that will be enclosed in an outside or carrier envelope in which the ballot and its envelope are to be returned. Usually the voter is instructed to take the ballots and affidavit to a notary public or other officer authorized to administer oaths, and in the presence of that officer, to mark his ballot —without, however, divulging to the officer how he votes. The ballot is then deposited in the official carrier envelope, which is then sealed. In some states, the notary public is required to place his seal on the voucher envelope, in others on the carrier envelope—these minor violations should be checked for each state. The envelope is then mailed, preferably by registered or certified mail, to the appropriate election official, or in some states it may be delivered in person or by an agent if this proves more convenient for the voter. In most cases, the ballot must arrive at the office of the registrar or election board in time to be delivered to the appropriate polling place before the polls close on election day. Some states, however, require that absentee ballots be in the hands of the election officers several days before the election; the voter should check carefully the regulations for his particular state. If an absentee ballot arrives after the prescribed deadline, it is marked to indicate its invalidity and placed in a special box or file without being opened. All such ballots are kept for several months after an election in case any investigation of the validity of the vote is undertaken.

Various techniques are employed to ensure the honesty of the balloting. In most states, absentee ballots are specially numbered and often the voucher and carrier envelopes are correspondingly numbered. Thus it is possible to check not only the authenticity of the ballot which is marked but also which of the absentee ballots are returned. In some states, of which Nevada is an example, if a voter applies for an absentee ballot but does not return it (that is, does not vote), his registration is cancelled, and he must re-register in order to recover his standing as a qualified elector. In states which clear registration lists of electors who do not vote for a period of years, it is necessary to keep track of which absentee voter does, in fact, cast his ballot and thus meets the qualification for consistent voting. The most conclusive check on the honesty of the ballot is, of course, the affidavit to which the voter swears when he fills out his ballot, for a voter is liable to conviction for perjury if he attests to false information on this voucher.

Either before the election or at the polls, an absentee ballot may be challenged on various grounds: establishing the falsity of information about voting qualifications, proving that the voter was not, in fact, absent from the voting district on election day or did not fulfill other necessary requirements, or showing that the absentee is not a registered voter in good standing. In case of challenge, the absentee ballot is put aside, the voter is notified that his vote has been challenged, and if possible he may appear to defend his right of franchise in person or may send the necessary information. It usually is not possible for a challenged absentee ballot to be verified by the voter on election day, but this is not of consequence unless the final count is so close as to be significantly changed by the absentee count.

In a number of states, if the elector casts an absentee ballot and then finds himself at home on election day—and therefore able to cast a ballot in person—he may vote at the polls provided the election officials have not completed their totaling of the absentee vote. If a voter dies after his absentee ballot has been cast, that ballot is not counted if the election officials receive information of the death in time to discount the vote.

PRE-ELECTION VOTING: Some states[1] arrange for voters who anticipate absence on election day to cast ballots at the office of the local election clerk before the regular election day. In states where this is possible, the voter may apply in person at the election office as soon as the ballots

---

[1] Alabama, Arizona, Arkansas, California, Colorado, Hawaii, Louisiana, Mississippi, Montana, Nebraska, North Dakota, Ohio, Oklahoma, Oregon, South Dakota, Tennessee, Texas, Vermont, West Virginia, and Wyoming.

are printed (usually several weeks before the election), receive his ballot and vote it on the spot in the presence of the election officer. Such ballots are held until election day when they are distributed to the appropriate polling place to be counted with the regularly-marked ballots. Actually in Mississippi, Alabama and Louisiana, this is the only way a voter may vote an absentee ballot. In Mississippi, the voter reports to the office of the Circuit Clerk (or the City Clerk in the case of a municipal election) between the tenth and second day before the election and casts his ballot at that time. In Alabama, the voter marks duplicate ballots with carbon paper in the presence of the County Register. The carbons are sent by registered mail daily to the Secretary of State—a unique check on the honesty of the election officer. In Louisiana one applies between the tenth and second day before an election, marks the ballot at the office of the Clerk of the District Court of the parish or at the office of the Civil Sheriff in the Parish of Orleans. In Montana, also, a "prospective absentee" may vote at the County Clerk's office any time after the official ballots have been printed. Similarly in Nebraska, anyone who expects to be absent may apply to the County Clerk or Election Commissioner, obtain a ballot and vote it provided he does so at least two full days before the election. In Ohio, similar provision is made for voters to cast an advance ballot at the Board of Elections, and in Oregon a voter may cast a ballot early provided he does it before 5 P.M. on the day before the election. The provisions for the other states usually follow similar patterns.

Military Absentee Voting[1]

The palpable need for some system of enfranchising soldiers, absent from their homes on election day because of military duty, led some states to adopt military absentee

[1] A detailed account of military absentee voting is found in **Voting in the Armed Forces,** Message from the President of the United States transmitting the Report of the Special Committee on Service Voting. (Washington, D. C.: Government Printing Office, 1952) House Document No. 407, 82d. Congress, 2d. sess.

voting provisions as early as the Civil War. At that time, 11 northern states provided through various laws that soldiers who were state residents could vote in the field or by proxy, and in the election of 1864 a fairly large number of soldiers received furloughs so that they could return home to vote. As the size of the armed forces serving overseas increased during the Spanish American War and then in the first World War, popular agitation increased for national absentee voting laws, but in neither conflict did Congress enact such legislation although absentee voting bills were introduced. By the beginning of World War II, a number of states had adopted laws which enabled servicemen to vote by absentee ballot, and in 1942 Congress passed the Servicemen's Voting Act which accorded soldiers the right to cast an absentee ballot for members of Congress and presidential electors and granted all servicemen exemption from any state requirements for personal registration or the payment of poll taxes in congressional or national elections. These congressional provisions were intended primarily to extend suffrage to servicemen coming from states without absentee voting regulations, but unfortunately the law was not passed until September, 1942 and therefore had little effect upon the number of servicemen actually participating in the 1942 election. In 1944, Congress amended the earlier legislation, strongly urged more state provisions, and provided a federal war ballot on which servicemen could vote for congressional candidates and presidential electors; but the attempts to provide a federal ballot proved highly unsatisfactory. The importance of providing for the military vote is suggested by statistics from the report by the American Political Science Association[1] which indicate that in 1944 there were 9,225,000 persons of voting age in the armed forces. Of that number, 4,487,540 applied for absentee ballots and 2,691,160 sent in ballots that were counted. Thus about 30 percent of the servicemen voted in comparison to 60 percent of the civilians of voting age who voted. The service vote com-

[1] **Voting in the Armed Forces,** p. 1.

prised about five and one-half percent of the total popular vote for President in 1944.

The various state laws operated during the war years with widely varying degrees of success in providing opportunity for military people to vote, and it became necessary after the war to provide for some peacetime guarantee of absentee voting rights for men still serving in the armed forces. However, persistent concern among some legislators and state officials that broadened federal legislation might threaten the power of the states to conduct their own elections prompted Congress in 1946 to pass legislation which essentially returned the control over absentee voting to the states. The 1946 law did, however, provide for a federal postcard on which application for an absentee ballot could be made to any state authority, and for special arrangements to facilitate the procurement and return of ballots by servicemen in remote areas. The federal law also continued the sections exempting soldiers from requirements for personal registration and for payment of poll taxes which might be imposed on civilians in their resident states.

The pervasive effect of the recommendations to the states which were contained in this congressional legislation is apparent in the more lenient provisions for military absentee voting found in most current state codes. The recommendations fall into three main parts. First, that the definition of the military voter should be expanded to include not only men in the actual fighting forces but also the wives and dependents who would share their overseas or out-of-state service in a peacetime army, as well as another sizable group of citizens serving in various religious and welfare groups attached to the armed forces. These included such groups as the United Service Organization, the American Red Cross, the Society of Friends, and the Salvation Army. Secondly, it was urged that more time should be allowed for obtaining and returning the ballots; in some states ballots were not available until less than a month before the election, and the experience during the 1940's showed that ballots could not be received, marked and returned to election officers in less than 45 days. States were therefore urged to provide absentee ballots at least 45 days, and preferably more, before election day. A third recommendation dealt with the problem of registration. Obviously servicemen could not register personally (although a few states still required personal registration in spite of congressional legislation eliminating it in national and congressional elections), and other state registration provisions were also difficult for servicemen to fulfill. It was recommended that either registration be waived entirely; or that the affidavit executed in applying for a ballot or in marking the ballot constitute registration; or that if special registration forms were required, they be sent to the voter with his ballot and be acceptable if returned with the ballot. Current state legislation shows implementation of these recommendations by an encouraging number of state legislatures.

ELIGIBILITY AND PROCEDURE FOR MILITARY ABSENTEE VOTING: As for the extension of absentee voting rights to wives and dependents of servicemen as well as to members of religious and welfare groups attached to the services, 34 states now have legislation with this broad coverage. The description (with only minor variations) reads as follows: members of the armed forces and the merchant marine (usually not including the men who serve on vessels on the inland waterways or the Great Lakes), and members of the womens' organizations such as the Women's Auxiliary Service Pilots, the Women's Naval Reserve, the Women's Auxiliary Corps, as well as members of the American Red Cross, the Salvation Army (only sometimes included), the United Service Organization, the Society of Friends and other welfare or religious organizations which are officially attached to the armed forces of the United States.

Laws in seven other states (Georgia, Illinois, Kansas, Massachusetts, Missouri, South Carolina and Texas) either omit the wives and dependents or members of welfare organizations from their definition of military voters, but include all of the other groups which have been recommended for inclusion. Texas makes one further exclusion: members of the regular military establishment.

In only nine states (Arizona, Arkansas, Hawaii, Nebraska, New Jersey, Ohio, Pennsylvania, Virginia, and West Virginia) is the definition of those eligible to cast a military ballot limited to electors in actual military service. In most of these, however, the civilian absent voting provisions seem broad enough to include the families of servicemen and other electors who may be working with the armed services in a civilian capacity.

In regard to the second problem, that of timing, an examination of existing statutes reveals that at least 35 states[1] now make military ballots available at least 40 days prior to any election. In most of the remaining states at least 30 days are allowed for the procurement and marking of absentee ballots.

The third criticism levelled at state provisions for absentee voting—that the requirements for registration were unnecessarily restrictive—has been met by the revision of registration provisions in a large number of states. In 11 states[2] registration has been waived for servicemen. In 19 states[3] the affidavit executed by the voter when he applies for an absentee ballot or the affidavit on the ballot envelope suffices as registration. Today, fewer than 20 states require registration as a separate act from the voting procedure.

Although there is still room for improvement in military voting procedures, the extent of the revision in the various states since the 1940's gives rise to optimism for the even-

---

[1] Alabama, Florida, Georgia, Idaho, Illinois, Indiana, Iowa, Maine, Maryland, Massachusetts, Michigan, Mississippi, Montana, Nebraska, Nevada, New Hampshire, New Mexico, New York, North Dakota, Ohio, Oklahoma, Oregon, Pennsylvania, Rhode Island, South Carolina, South Dakota, Tennessee, Texas, Utah, Vermont, Virginia, Washington, West Virginia, Wisconsin, and Wyoming.

[2] Illinois, Kansas, Maryland, Missouri, Ohio, Oklahoma, Rhode Island, Tennessee, Texas, Virginia, and Wisconsin.

[3] California, Delaware, Florida, Idaho, Indiana, Iowa, Kentucky, Michigan, Minnesota, Nebraska, Nevada, New Hampshire, New Mexico, New York, North Carolina, Oregon, Utah, Washington and Wyoming.

tual correction of the major problems in our military absentee voting system.

Concluding Comments

The striking increase in absent voting provisions in the United States, coming as it does in response to the mores —and mobility—of the electorate, is an encouraging sign of the adaptation of the election process to changed conditions. But the mere institution of such procedures is not enough. There must be careful and continuing surveillance on the part of election officials to make certain that the methods used are straightforward enough to be attractive to the maximum number of eligible voters yet complicated enough to maintain the honesty of the people's mandate.

NOTE TO READERS CONSULTING THE CHARTS ON STATE REQUIREMENTS: All of the state-by-state charts have been compiled by the author directly from the most recent available election codes for each state. Every effort has been made to check relevant session laws to ensure that the data are accurate up to December, 1959. The recent January, 1960 Pennsylvania provisions regarding absentee voting are also included.

APPENDIX
CHART I
LITERACY REQUIREMENTS

ALABAMA:
Read and write article of United States Constitution in English. Exemption is given to owner (or his spouse) of 40 acres of land or real estate or personal property assessed for taxation at $300, if the taxes on such property are paid.*

ALASKA:
Voter must be able to read in English the United States Constitution and to write in English unless voter at general election of November 4, 1924.*

ARIZONA:
Write name and read from United States Constitution in English without being prompted or reciting from memory.*

CALIFORNIA:
Read Constitution in English and write name unless voter on October 10, 1911 or over 60 years old.*

CONNECTICUT:
Read in English at least three lines of any article of Constitution or any section of statutes of Connecticut without being prompted or reciting from memory. Voter who has defective sight or is blind must be able to write an article of Constitution from dictation or read in Braille.

DELAWARE:
Read Delaware constitution in English and write name if became 21 or a citizen after January 1, 1900.*

GEORGIA:
Read aloud "intelligibly" and write "legibly" in English a section of Georgia or United States Constitution. Or may qualify on basis of "good character and an understanding of the duties and obligations of citizenship under a republican form of government;" such understanding to be demonstrated by answering correctly 20 out of 30 standard questions which are included in the law. Three sample questions are: 1) What is a republican form of government; 2) What is the definition of a felony in Georgia; 3) What do the Constitutions of the United States and of Georgia provide regarding the suspension of the privilege of the writ of Habeas Corpus?

HAWAII:
Read and write English or Hawaiian.

LOUISIANA:
Read and give a reasonable interpretation of any clause in Louisiana or United States Constitution and write own applica-

65

tion in English or by dictation in "mother tongue" without assistance from any person or any memorandum. If claim physical disability must have 2 qualified electors of his precinct attest to oath of physical disability or inability to write English. Or, if applicant cannot read and write may register if of good character, attached to principles of the constitution and can give reasonable interpretation of any section of either constitution when read to him.*

MAINE:
Write name and read Maine constitution in English without being prompted or reciting from memory.*

MASSACHUSETTS:
Read constitution of Commonwealth in English and write name. Registrar has slips printed with five lines of constitution; applicant draws one from box and reads it aloud.*

MISSISSIPPI:
Read any section of state constitution or if unable to read, must be able to understand and give reasonable interpretation of a section when read to him. Must complete written application for registration.

NEW HAMPSHIRE:
Read and write without being assisted or reciting from memory unless had right to vote on January 1, 1904. Uniform pasteboard slips printed with five lines of constitution are placed in box; applicant draws one and reads aloud lines printed on it and writes one of lines and signs name in presence of supervisors.*

NEW YORK:
Read and write English if gained right to vote after January 1, 1922. Ability to read and write English tested by Board of Regents. In districts with personal registration, voter presents certificate of literacy; in districts of non-personal registration, voter may be given literacy test by election inspectors on election and registration days only. New voter may present literacy certificate or diploma showing he has completed 8th grade or high school or a matriculation card issued by a college or university. Veteran may present certificate of honorable discharge as proof of literacy.*

NORTH CAROLINA:
Read and write any section of state constitution in English. North Carolina constitution states that no male person eligible to vote in any state on January 1, 1867, or a "lineal descendant" of such person, shall be denied right to register and vote because of failure to pass this test, provided he was registered before December 1, 1908.

OREGON:

Read and write English by reading paragraph of own choosing from any available printed matter and by signing name.*

SOUTH CAROLINA:

Read and write any section of state constitution submitted by registration officer. Or, show that own and have paid all taxes collectible during previous year on property in South Carolina assessed at $300 or more.

VIRGINIA:

Make application to register in own handwriting without aid, suggestion or memorandum.*

WASHINGTON:

Read and speak English unless voter in Washington on November 3, 1896. May be asked to read aloud and explain meaning of some ordinary English prose.

WYOMING:

Read constitution of state.*

---

* All states so designated either exempt completely or have special literacy tests for the physically disabled voter.

CHART II

POLL TAX REQUIREMENTS

ALABAMA:

Pay poll tax ($1.50) between October 1 and February 1. Poll tax must be paid for two preceding years. Members of armed forces and honorably discharged veterans are exempt.

ARKANSAS:

Pay poll tax ($1.00) between October 2 and October 1 of following year. Members of armed forces and voters who become 21 after poll tax assessed are exempt.

MISSISSIPPI:

If between 21 and 60 years of age, pay poll tax ($2.00) by February 1; must also show proof of payment of poll tax for two preceding years in order to vote. Members of armed forces or attached service agencies and their wives, and persons who are deaf and dumb, or blind, or maimed by loss of hand or foot are exempt. Poll tax may be paid by an agent.

TEXAS:

If between 21 and 60 years of age, pay poll tax ($1.75) between October 1 and February 1. Those who will become 21 after February 1, or Indians not taxed, or blind, deaf or dumb persons, or those who have lost a hand or foot, and all veterans with forty percent disability are exempt.

VIRGINIA:
Pay poll tax ($1.50) at least six months before general election. New voter must pay poll taxes for previous three years unless he has just moved into state or has just become 21. Members of armed forces who are overseas are exempt.

CHART III

REGISTRATION AND TRANSFER REQUIREMENTS

Note: For all states, "Personal" refers to registration in person; "Absentee" refers to registration by mail. The provisions listed under "Transfer" give the regulations for changing registration in case of change of address, change of name, or the wish to change one's party affiliation. The phrase "no provision found" means that the author has been unable to find a pertinent provision in the state election code, but that some provision may exist. The phrase "no provision" indicates that there is no arrangement for such registration.

ALABAMA
PERSONAL: Apply to Board of Registrars at court house on 1st and 3rd Mondays of each month but not within 10 days of election. May be additional sessions for registration. Voter receives certificate of registration.
ABSENTEE: No provision.
TRANSFER:
Address: If move from 1 precinct or ward to another in same county within 3 months before election, may vote in former precinct at next election. If move from 1 county to another, re-register.
Name: Apply to Board of Registrars.
Party Affiliation: No provision for transfer.

ALASKA
No pre-registration. Signing of register at polls by elector himself, or for him at his request by judge of election, apparently constitutes registration as qualified voter.

ARIZONA
PERSONAL: In incorporated cities and towns, apply to City or Town Clerk; in other areas apply to County Recorder, Justice of the Peace, or Deputy Registrar. Register for primary any time up to 5 P.M. of day 4 months before general election; register for general election any time up to 5 P.M. of the 6th Monday before general election.

ABSENTEE: If absent from state, apply to County Recorder, have registration application notarized and return to Recorder. Voters in incorporated cities and towns not included in this provision.

TRANSFER:

Address: If move from one precinct to another while registration closed, may vote in former precinct until registration re-opens. If move while registration open, re-register.

Name: Re-register.

Party Affiliation: Re-register.

ARKANSAS

No registration system. Anyone paying poll tax is eligible to vote provided otherwise qualified. Pay poll tax ($1.00) in person or by mail or through member of family to County Collector from October 2 up to and including October 1 of next year. Tax receipts issued.

CALIFORNIA

PERSONAL: Apply to County Clerk or Registrar of Voters in Los Angeles, San Diego and San Francisco counties. Register any time up to 53 days before election.

Special provision for "new registrants": If have resided in California at least 54 days before presidential election, apply in person or by mail between 90th and 45th day before election at County Clerk's office for "new registrant" standing. Mark presidential ballot in person not more than 5 nor less than 1 day before election. Submit certificate from election officer in former out-of-state residence.

ABSENTEE: If absent from county, obtain from County Clerk or Registrar of Voters Affidavit of Registration in duplicate. Fill out, have notarized and return form in duplicate to County Clerk by registered or certified mail whenever possible.

TRANSFER:

Address: If move from one precinct to another within county while registration open, transfer registration to new precinct. If move outside county, execute Affidavit of Cancellation and deliver it to registration officer in new county.

Name: If change name through marriage, change registration at polls by signing maiden name, then married name. If name changed by court order, re-register.

Party Affiliation: Apply to County Clerk or Registrar of Voters before close of registration.

COLORADO

PERSONAL: If resident of outlying precinct, or precinct in cities and towns which are not county seats, or in precinct in cities of over 100,000, apply to Registration Committee appointed by County Clerk for each precinct on publicized registration days or apply to County Clerk. If resident of other election precinct or of county seat, apply only in person at office of County Clerk any time after 45 days following general election up to and including Monday, 15th day before primary or election.

Special provision: Elector already registered and personally known to County Clerk or his deputy, may register any member of his family, including servants, who are qualified electors and reside at same address.

ABSENTEE: File or have filed with County Clerk or Election Commission a verified application for registration on official form any time after 45 days following general state election up to and including 20th day before primary, general or special election.

TRANSFER:

Address: If move from one precinct to another within county while registration open, change registration in person or by verified written application to County Clerk. Elector known to Clerk can transfer address for all family members. If move from one county to another within 90 days or from one precinct to another within 15 days before primary or general election, may vote by absentee ballot or at polling place in county or precinct where registered. If move within precinct, notify County Clerk, or make transfer with judges of election on election day.

Name: No provision found.

Party Affiliation: Apply in person to Registration Committee at first registration session in any primary election year. Or apply in writing to any member of Registration Committee at least 1 day before registration day. Or apply in person to County Clerk or Election Commission any time in any primary year up to and including Saturday, 10th day before primary.

CONNECTICUT

PERSONAL: Apply to Board of Registrars during regular sessions held for "admission of electors"; usually in session from Saturday of 6th week until Saturday of 4th week before regular election.

ABSENTEE: No provision for civilians.

TRANSFER:

Address: If move before 1st day of month before election, name will be removed from registry list unless elector obtains continuance or transfer of registration. If move from one municipality to another may vote in former municipality for 1 day less than 6 months afterward, provided elector presents to Registrars of former municipality request in writing for continuance of registration not later than 7 days before state election. In municipalities over 5,000 submit signed application for transfer of registration.

Name: If change name through marriage can vote under maiden name, if can prove identity; Registrars will correct registry list at polls. Or write to Registrar any time up to 6 days before election.

Party Affiliation: Apply in writing to Registrar to have name removed from enrollment list or transferred to list of another party. Cannot vote in caucus or primary of party to which transferred for 6 months from date of transfer application.

DELAWARE
PERSONAL: Apply to Registration Officers of election district on 3rd Wednesday in July, 1st Saturday in August or 3rd Saturday in October before election in even-numbered years. Additional registration days provided; notices posted.

ABSENTEE: No provision for civilians.

TRANSFER:

Address: If move from one election district to another, apply in person to Department having custody of county registration records any time before last day of registration. Or apply in person to Registration Officers in election district on registration days. If move within county when registration closed, voter may vote if properly identified at polls. If move from one county to another, apply to Department in either former or new county for transfer.

Name: Re-register and authorize cancellation of previous registration. If name change occurs when registration closed, may vote at next election.

Party Affiliation: Apply on official form to Department any time before 3rd Wednesday of July.

FLORIDA
FOR COUNTIES WITHOUT PERMANENT REGISTRATION: Consult local boards for regulations.

FOR COUNTIES WITH PERMANENT REGISTRATION: Registration certificates issued. If under 21 and subject to induction, apply any time to Supervisor of Registration; registration becomes official when voter reaches 21. Other voters apply to Supervisor of Registration any time except 30 days before and 5 days after election.

ABSENTEE: No provision for civilians.

TRANSFER:

Address: If move from one precinct to another, notify Supervisor and obtain Certificate of Transfer. If move from one county to another, re-register and request cancellation of old registration.

Name: Notify Supervisor.

Party Affiliation: Apply any time registration open after general election and 30 days before next primary.

GEORGIA
PERSONAL: Apply to Registrar or deputy in office at courthouse any time but may not register to vote in election for General Assembly later than 6 months before that election. Registration office open at least one day a week.

ABSENTEE: No provision found.

TRANSFER:

Address: If move to another county, apply to Board of Registrars of former county for Registration Transfer Certificate. After obtaining Certificate, apply to Board of Registrars of new county at least 10 days before election. If move within county, notify Board of Registrars.

Name: Report to Registrar.

Party Affiliation: No provision found.

HAWAII

PERSONAL: Apply to County Clerk any time except from 3rd Wednesday before to general election and from 5th Friday before to special or primary election.

ABSENTEE: If unable to register in person, secure blank affidavit from County Clerk and have it notarized. Voter's affidavit must be supported by affidavits of at least 3 electors who know applicant.

TRANSFER:

Address: If move from one precinct or county to another, re-register with County Clerk.

Name: No provision found.

Party Affiliation: Party affiliation not recorded on registration.

IDAHO

PERSONAL: Apply to Registrar of precinct from 1st Monday of March up to 9 P.M. on last Saturday before primary and after primary up to 9 P.M. on last Saturday before general election. Husband or wife can register for spouse if elector personally known to Registrar.

Interim registration: Elector to be absent during regular registration periods may register in person before Clerk of Board of County Commissioners any time during "interim."

ABSENTEE: If absent from precinct during registration period, apply in writing to Clerk of Board of County Commissioners for "Elector's Oath"; have it notarized and forward to Clerk before registration closes.

TRANSFER:

Address: If move while registration open, apply in person or by registered mail to have name stricken from register. Registrar will send Transfer Certificate, entitling elector to registration in new precinct if it is filed before registration closes. Submit Transfer Certificate in person or by registered mail. Or re-register in new precinct.

Name: No provision found.

Party Affiliation: Party affiliation not recorded on registration.

ILLINOIS

COUNTIES OF LESS THAN 500,000 POPULATION:

PERSONAL: Apply in person to County Clerk any time except 28 days before and 2 days after election. May register in precinct on announced days before election.

ABSENTEE: No provision for civilians.

TRANSFER:
Address: If move within precinct may transfer address with judges of election. If move within county, apply to County Clerk for transfer up to 28 days before election.
Name: Re-register and authorize cancellation of old registration. If change name within 2 year period before election, may change record with election judges.
Party Affiliation: May not change party affiliation within 23 months of next primary.
FOR COUNTIES OF MORE THAN 500,000 POPULATION:
PERSONAL: Apply to County Clerk or Board of Election Commissioners in Chicago any time except 28 days before and 2 days after election. Offices of city, town or village clerks also open from 1st Monday of May until 3rd Monday of September and from 3rd Tuesday of November to 3rd Tuesday of January of each year and on March 1, 2 and 3 of each year. May also register in precinct on announced days.
ABSENTEE: No provision for civilians.
TRANSFER:
Address: If move within county, apply in writing on official form or in person to County Clerk any time up to 28 days before election. If move when registration closed, may vote by presenting to election judges affidavit of change with supporting affidavit of a qualified voter who is a householder in same precinct.
Name: Re-register and authorize cancellation of old registration. If change name when registration closed, may vote in next election by signing affidavit at polls.
Party Affiliation: May not change party affiliation within 23 months of next primary.

INDIANA
PERSONAL: Apply to Clerk of Circuit Court in counties of less than 80,000 or to Board of Registration in other counties any time from 1st secular day of December of general election year until 29th day before county or city primary and from May 15 to 29th day before general or city election.
ABSENTEE: Voter absent from county until after time for registering for ensuing election may execute affidavit for registration before anyone authorized to administer oaths. May not register within 29 days before election. Physically disabled voter may register by having affidavit notarized. (Physician's certificate required.)
TRANSFER:
Address: Mail registration receipt from last registration to Clerk or Registration Board and request on back of receipt the transfer desired.
Name: Notify Clerk or Registration Board.
Party Affiliation: If voted for majority of regularly nominated can-

didate of party at last preceding general election, voter may participate in that party's primary, or if did not vote in last general election, but intend to vote for party in forthcoming election, may participate in that primary. Party affiliation is recorded with name in poll-list.

IOWA

CITIES WITH PERMANENT REGISTRATION:

PERSONAL: Apply to Commissioner of Registration up to and including 10th day before election.

ABSENTEE: Voter permanently disabled or to be absent from election precinct until after next election may apply in writing to Commissioner of Registration (in Des Moines) for duplicate registration cards. Have notarized and return any time up to and including 10th day before election.

TRANSFER:

Address: If change residence not later than 10 days before election, obtain removal notice from Commissioner of Registration. Complete form and return it; may then vote in new precinct. If residence changed within 10 days of election, vote in former precinct.

Name: Re-register.

Party Affiliation: File written declaration with County Auditor up to 10 days before primary. If not previously registered or if party affiliation not recorded, or if have changed from one precinct to another, may vote in primary by declaring affiliation at polls.

CITIES WITHOUT PERMANENT REGISTRATION:

PERSONAL: Apply to Registers at regular voting places on:
1) 2nd Thursday before general, city or special election. In nonpresidential years, session lasts 2 days (Thursday and Friday); in presidential years, 3 days (Thursday, Friday, and Saturday).
2) last Saturday before election.
3) election day for anyone who has been absent on days fixed for registration or for naturalized citizen who has received final papers since last preceding registration day.

New registry taken in each presidential year. On affidavit brought by registered elector, Registers will visit a sick elector and register him.

ABSENTEE: No provision found for absentee registration *per se*; however, for voter casting absentee ballot, affidavit upon ballot envelope apparently constitutes sufficient registration of voter in precincts where registration is required.

TRANSFER:

Address: Apply in person to Registers during regular registration session.

Name: Apply in person to Registers during regular registration session.

Party Affiliation: Same as for cities with permanent registration.

KANSAS

PERSONAL: Apply to City Clerk or Election Commissioner (in counties having more than 90,000 population). Check times for registration with local officials.

ABSENTEE: In cities of 1st and 2nd class, elector who cannot appear in person may register by mail. Apply to City Clerk or Election Commissioner on official form which has been notarized. In all areas anyone sick or physically disabled (physician's certificate required) may apply to Election Commissioner or City Clerk to register by mail.

TRANSFER:

Address: Report change to City Clerk or Election Commissioner. May be required to re-register in certain areas.

Name: Notify City Clerk or Election Commissioner.

Party Affiliation: Apply to County Clerk up to 30 days before primary.

KENTUCKY

PERSONAL: Apply to County Clerk or Board of Registration Commissioners or branch of Board if live in city of 1st class. Registration closed 59 days before and 5 days after primary or general election and 10 days before special election.

ABSENTEE: No provision for residents living outside of cities of 1st class. No provision found for cities of 1st class.

TRANSFER:

Address: In city of 1st class, if move from one precinct to another apply to Board of Registration Commissioners. Outside cities of 1st class, if move from one precinct to another within county, apply in person or in writing to County Clerk.

Name: In all localities, re-register.

Party Affiliation: In all localities apply in person or by mail during registration to County Clerk or Board of Registration Commissioners. Must have been registered member of declared party at time of preceding regular election to vote in primary or if new registrant, must have been registered and remained registered as member of that party.

LOUISIANA

PERSONAL: Apply to Registrar of Voters of parish any time up to 30 days before election.

ABSENTEE: No provision for civilians.

TRANSFER:

Address: In cities with permanent registration: If move within parish, any time before election (including 30 days before) apply in person or in writing to Registrar. Except Registrar of New Orleans is specifically prohibited from making address changes between 1st and 2nd primaries. If move from one precinct to another within parish may vote in former precinct for 3 months.

Name: Re-register except during 30 days before election.
Party Affiliation: Write Registrar requesting change of affiliation. May not vote in any primary for 6 months.

MAINE

PERSONAL: Apply to Board of Registration or City Clerk. In cities over 30,000 Board of Registration in session every day except 12 days before election. In other cities, check hours when Board is in session.

ABSENTEE: No provision except: On written request certified in writing by attending physician, member of Registration Board will go to home of physically disabled voter within 20 miles of registration office for purpose of registering him. And if person becomes 21 between last day of open registration session and close of polls, his name may be added to registration lists at any time *without personal appearance.*

TRANSFER:

Address: Notify City Clerk or Board of Registration in writing or in person. If residence changed after April 1, change will be made on voting list, but not on registration list; therefore, voter should vote in ward or precinct in which he resided on April 1.

Name: Apply in person to Board of Registration or City Clerk and re-register. If name changed after registration closed, may present marriage certificate or court document to Board at polls.

Party Affiliation: Apply to Board of Registration; may not vote in political caucus or primary for 6 months thereafter. If not enrolled in a party, may enroll at time of primary by taking oath.

MARYLAND

IN BALTIMORE CITY, AND ALLEGANY, ANNE ARUNDEL, DORCHESTER, FREDERICK, MONTGOMERY, PRINCE GEORGE'S AND WASHINGTON COUNTIES, AND OTHER COUNTIES WITH PERMANENT REGISTRATION:

Register, transfer, affiliate or change affiliation at office of Board of Supervisors of Elections any time except 30 days before and 10 days after primary or special election and 42 days before and 15 days after a general election. May not change party affiliation during 6 months before and 10 days following primary or 42 days before and 15 days following a general or special election.

No provisions for absentee registration.

IN ALL OTHER COUNTIES:

Check special arrangements for registration.

MASSACHUSETTS

PERSONAL: Apply to Board of Registrars (sometimes called Board of Election Commissioners) any time except 31 days before and day after biennial state primary, presidential primary, and biennial state election and 19 days before and day after city election or annual town meeting.

ABSENTEE: Physically disabled elector may apply in writing not later than 3rd day before last day for registration. 2 Registrars, representing different parties, will register voter at home.

TRANSFER:

Address: Residence on January 1 used for voting purposes throughout the year. If change address, notify Board of Registrars or Board of Election Commissioners.

Name: Notify Board of Registrars. May vote under former name until succeeding January 1.

Party Affiliation: If not listed by party on voter list, may declare party to clerk at primary. Cannot change enrollment during 31 days before primary; at other times, apply in person to Board of Registrars.

MICHIGAN

PERSONAL: Apply to Township, City or Village Clerk any time up to and including 30th day before any election.

ABSENTEE: If physically disabled or absent from township, obtain duplicate registration cards from Town Clerk, have them notarized and return to Clerk.

TRANSFER:

Address: If move while registration open, apply in writing or in person to Clerk for Transfer of Registration. If move from one precinct to another within same district, transfer registration on election day by applying to election board with which registered. If request is accepted, elector can then vote in former precinct for that election *only*.

Name: No provision found.

Party Affiliation: No provision found.

MINNESOTA

PERSONAL: Apply to Commissioner of Registration up to 20 days before election.

ABSENTEE: If absent from election district, apply by mail to Commissioner up to 20 days before election.

TRANSFER:

Address: If move from one precinct to another within municipality more than 30 days before election, submit removal notice by mail or in person to Commissioner of Registration. If move from one place to another in same district, no removal notice need be filed.

Name: Re-register.

Party Affiliation: No provision found.

MISSISSIPPI

PERSONAL: Apply any time to County Registrar; must register at least 4 months before general election to vote in that election and in immediately preceding primary.

ABSENTEE: No provision.
TRANSFER:
Address: If move from one precinct to another, re-register after residence of 1 year at new address.
Name: No provision found.
Party Affiliation: No provision found for legally transferring party affiliation. If voter challenged at primary, he must answer oath that he is in accord with principles enunciated by state convention of his party.

MISSOURI
Since there are separate and different provisions for registration for various cities and counties, voter is referred to election code or to his local registration offices.

MONTANA
PERSONAL: Apply to County Clerk up to 45-day period before election. All notaries and justices of the peace are designated Deputy Registrars in county where they reside and are qualified to register voters who live more than 10 miles from County Clerk's office.
ABSENTEE: If absent from county apply by mail to County Clerk for Registration Card; have it notarized and return to County Clerk or Deputy Registrar before close of registration. 2 registered electors must appear before County Clerk and swear to validity of applicant's signature on absentee application.
Physically disabled elector may request in writing to County Clerk that registration be made at residence.
TRANSFER:
Address: If move from one precinct to another within county, execute Registry Card in person before Deputy Registrar of new precinct or notary or justice of the peace within county, or notify County Clerk in writing on official form. Elector living outside incorporated city or town may change precinct if one more convenient than another to his residence. If move from one county to another, re-register.
Name: No provision found.
Party Affiliation: May not change affiliation in same primary. No provision found for official transfer.

NEBRASKA
COUNTIES OVER 60,000:
PERSONAL: Apply to Election Commissioner any time up to 5 P.M. on Friday before election. Other registration places may be provided.
ABSENTEE: No provision found.
TRANSFER:
Address: If move from one voting district to another, re-register.
Name: Re-register.

78

Party Affiliation: No provision found except for change of affiliation by prospective candidate.

CITIES OF 7,000-40,000:

PERSONAL: Revision of registration held immediately before general election in November of each year.

ABSENTEE: No provision found.

TRANSFER: No provisions found for transfer of address, name or party affiliation.

NEVADA

PERSONAL: Apply to County Clerk or Deputy Registrar (all justices of the peace except those located in county seats are deputy registrars) up to 30 days before election.

ABSENTEE: No provision for civilians.

TRANSFER:

Address: If move from one precinct to another within county, re-register. If move when registration closed, residence is not lost in former country or precinct.

Name: Re-register.

Party Affiliation: Re-register any time before closing hour for declaration of candidacy before primary.

NEW HAMPSHIRE

PERSONAL: Apply to Board of Election Supervisors at periodic sessions held between April 1 and August 1 in even-numbered years. Consult local Election Supervisor for exact registration dates.

ABSENTEE: No provision found.

TRANSFER:

Address: Retain right to vote in town or ward of previous residence for period of 6 months before election. Obtain Transfer Card not more than 6 months nor less than 5 days before election, present Transfer Card in new voting district, and vote.

Name: Notify Board of Election Supervisors.

Party Affiliation: Appear in person before Supervisors of town not less than 90 days before primary. Must state under oath intention to affiliate with and generally support candidates of party with which affiliating. If not previously affiliated with a party, may do so at time of primary.

NEW JERSEY

PERSONAL: Apply to County Board of Elections or duly appointed registration clerk up to and including 40th day before election.

ABSENTEE: If unable to register in person due to chronic or incurable illness, or physical disability (physician's certificate required), may be registered at home or place of confinement. No other provision for absentee registration.

TRANSFER:

Address: If move within county, notify in writing or in person the County Board of Elections or Municipal Clerk (if residence not in county seat). If move after registration closed, vote in former district.

Name: Re-register. If name changed after registration closed, vote under former name in election, but re-register for subsequent elections.

Party Affiliation: If vote in primary of one political party, considered member of that party until 2 subsequent annual primary elections have elapsed. If voter has not voted in primary for 2 annual elections he may not vote in any primary until he has first filed a declaration designating his party with the District Board. Considered member of a party if have been elected or appointed to public or party office, or have contributed toward campaign funds within 1 year of a primary.

NEW MEXICO

PERSONAL: Apply to County Clerk any time except after 5 P.M. on 30th day before election to Monday following election.

ABSENTEE: If temporarily out of county or state during registration period, write to County Clerk for Affidavit of Registration. Execute form in triplicate and forward by registered or certified mail to Clerk within regular registration period.

TRANSFER:

Address: If move within county, apply in writing to County Clerk up to 30 days before election. If move from one county to another, re-register in person with County Clerk and request cancellation of former registration.

Name: Apply to County Clerk or have application for change notarized and file with County Clerk.

Party Affiliation: Change in party affiliation must be notarized. Cannot change or designate party affiliation after Governor has issued proclamation for primary until after primary, and then only until 30th day before any other election at which registration is required.

NEW YORK

PERSONAL: Since the state of New York has adopted new laws (1957, 1958 and 1959) which provide for different local and central registration periods for: 1) counties with permanent personal registration, 2) counties in their first year of a permanent personal registration system, and 3) counties which have not adopted a permanent personal registration system, consult local Board of Elections for specific hours and days for local and central registration in voter's resident district.

TRANSFER:

Address: Notify County Central Registration Board or Veterans' Absentee Registration Board or apply in person to Board of

Inspectors of former election district during local registration days.

Name: The court which authorizes a name change reports directly to appropriate Board of Elections and registration is corrected.

Party Affiliation: Apply in person (or in special cases by mail) to Board of Elections any time from January 1 to 30th day preceding fall primary, except during 30 days preceding a spring primary. Change of party enrollment may be made only once in a year.

NORTH CAROLINA

COUNTIES HAVING ONE OR MORE MUNICIPALITIES OF OVER 10,000 WITH PERMANENT REGISTRATION:

PERSONAL: Apply any time to home or office of Registrar up to 21 days before election.

ABSENTEE: Apply to County Commissioners.

TRANSFER:

Address: If move from one precinct or ward to another, file affidavit with County Board or Registrar up to 21 days before primary or general election.

Name: No provision found.

Party Affiliation: File affidavit of change with County Board of Elections not less than 21 days before primary.

OTHER AREAS:

PERSONAL: Apply to local Registrar from 4th Saturday to 2nd Saturday before primary or general election. Registrar's office officially open on 4th, 3rd, and 2nd Saturdays in this period for registration, but on other days Registrar must keep books open at his home. If voter becomes eligible to register after registration closed, register on election day.

Special Provision: If absent from precinct during registration period, register with chairman of County Board of Elections before registration period. May register on day of 2nd primary, provided have attained qualifications to register since 1st primary. May vote in 1st primary if will be qualified to vote in general election.

ABSENTEE: No provision found.

TRANSFER:

Address: If move from one precinct to another, re-register and authorize cancellation of former registration. If move less than 30 days before general election, vote in that election in former precinct.

Name: No provision found.

Party Affiliation: Apply to Registrar of precinct during regular registration.

NORTH DAKOTA

PERSONAL: In cities and villages over 1,500, apply to Board of

Registration on Tuesday before general election. No registration required to vote in primaries.
ABSENTEE: No provision found.
TRANSFER:
Address: If move from one precinct to another, vote in former precinct until residence in new precinct established.
Name: No provision found.
Party Affiliation: No provision found.

OHIO

PERSONAL: Registration required in all cities over 16,000. Apply in person at Board of Elections any time except after 9 P.M. of 41st day before primary or general election or after 4 P.M. on 11th day before special election and 10 days after any election.
ABSENTEE: If will be unavoidably absent and more than 50 miles from precinct during registration period, file affidavit with Clerk of Election Board. Physically disabled voter, or voter prevented by illness from registering during regular period, may apply to Board for registration forms. These should be completed and, together with an affidavit of disability, should be delivered to Clerk or Registrar by an elector who can give sworn testimony on facts involved.
TRANSFER:
Address: If move while registration open, register change of address in person or in writing with Board of Elections. If move from one precinct or county to another after close of registration, vote in former precinct for that election. If move within precinct, may vote and poll officials will change registration.
Name: Re-register. If name changed within 48 days of election, vote at that election under former name, but re-register before voting at subsequent election.
Party Affiliation: Political affiliation determined by voter's sworn statement as to his voting in most recent state election. Must give oath that voted at that election for majority of candidates of party affiliation claimed. If did not vote at that election, may declare affiliation under oath at primary.

OKLAHOMA

PERSONAL: Apply to Secretary of County Election Board any time except 10 days before and 5 days after election, or apply to Precinct Registrar not less than 10 nor more than 30 days before election. Voter will receive voter's identification card. New registration required for all voters after January 1, 1959.
ABSENTEE: No provision.
TRANSFER:
Address: If move from one precinct to another, submit in person or by mail official form along with voter's identification card to Secretary of County Election Board or Precinct Registrar.

If move to new county, re-register.

Name: Notify County Election Board or Precinct Registrar.

Party Affiliation: May not change affiliation during period from 5 P.M. April 1 through 5 P.M. August 1 of even-numbered years, and from 5 P.M. February 1 through 5 P.M. May 1 of all odd-numbered years. At other times apply to County Election Board.

OREGON

PERSONAL: Apply to County Clerk or official Registrar any time up to 30 days before election. If will complete residence requirement or become 21 when registration closed, register during 30 days preceding close of registration.

ABSENTEE: Register in county other than home county and registration will be forwarded to county of residence. If absent from state, register before an official with electoral registration function, sign sworn statement verifying registration information and mail statement with certification of election official to County Clerk in home county.

TRANSFER:

Address: If move from one precinct or county to another while registration open, re-register in person or by mail with County Clerk. If move while registration closed, obtain from County Clerk of former district certificate of registration which allows elector to vote *once* after change of residence.

Name: Re-register.

Party Affiliation: Apply to County Clerk. May not change affiliation within 30 days before or on day of primary.

PENNSYLVANIA

PERSONAL: Apply any time to Registration Commission (or established branches) or on designated days to Registrar in district or ward. Register any time except election day or the 50 days before each general, municipal or primary election, and the 30 days after each election and 5 days after each primary. Special local registration boards may be provided.

ABSENTEE: No provision for civilians.

TRANSFER:

Address: If move from one address to another in same district, at least 10 days before primary or general election, mail removal notice on official form to Commission. 2 registered electors of new district must sign. Or apply in person to Registration Commission.

Name: No provision found.

Party Affiliation: Apply in person on official "change of party enrollment" form any time except 50 days before and 30 days after primary to Commission or to Registrars in ward or district. Cannot change party enrollment between primary and next general election or more than once between any November election and next primary.

RHODE ISLAND

PERSONAL: Apply to local Board of Canvassers any time except 60 days before election.

ABSENTEE: Shut-in voter apply in writing to local board, fill out official form, have it notarized or signed by 2 witnesses, and return to Board of Canvassers. Board will send final registration forms.

TRANSFER:

Address: If move within voting district, file written request with local board any time before election day, or file with Moderator or Warden of voting district on election day. If move within city or town, but to different voting district, request transfer of registration any time before election. If move to different city, re-register, except voter retains right to vote in former city for 1 day less than 6 months before election.

Name: Notify Board of Canvassers.

Party Affiliation: Notify Board of Canvassers. Cannot participate in primary of another political party until 26 months after participation in primary of competing party.

SOUTH CAROLINA

PERSONAL: Apply to Board of Registration at County Court House. Registration books open on 1st Monday of each month and during election years open for 3 successive days each month. In general election year, books open during the first 15 days of May and August. Other registration sessions may be held. Registration closed for 30 days before any election until after the election, and also closed before June primary until after second primary.

ABSENTEE: No provision for civilians.

TRANSFER:

Address: If move from one precinct or county to another, notify Board of Registration in new location, surrender Certificate of Registration, and request transfer of registration and new certificate.

Name: No provision found.

Party Affiliation: No provision found.

SOUTH DAKOTA

PERSONAL: Apply in person to City Auditor or Town Clerk or other authorized Board of Registration from September 1 before general election up to and including Tuesday before election.

ABSENTEE: No provision found.

TRANSFER:

Address: Apply to Board of Registration at time of regular biennial registration.

Name: Notify Board of Registration.

Party Affiliation: Notify Board of Registration.

REGISTRATION FOR PRIMARY ELECTIONS: If no change in residence or political affiliation, County Auditor will continue registration as of most recent primary. All others register in person at County Auditor's office, or procure registration card, complete, and forward to County Auditor at last 15 days before primary.

TENNESSEE

PERSONAL: Apply to County Election Commission any time except the 20 days before election in counties of 25,000 or more; or any time except the 10 days before election in counties of less than 25,000. A 2-day supplemental session may be held 20 days before election in areas remote from county seat. Special provisions for registration outside home county if occupation or service for state makes absence necessary.

ABSENTEE: If absent from residence by reason of regular occupation or business, register by mail. Request registration form from County Election Commission, have it notarized and return by registered mail to Commission before close of registration. If incapacitated by illness or other causes, ask County Election Commission to send Registrar-at-Large to home to register voter.

TRANSFER:

Address: If move from one precinct or county to another, transfer registration by written application on official forms to County Commissioner of Elections. Change of address must be made before the 20 or 10 day deadline before elections.

Name: Re-register.

Party Affiliation: No provision found.

TEXAS

PERSONAL: Texas does not have regular registration as such; the poll tax list is used as voter list. Poll tax is collected from every person between 21 and 60 who resided in state on January 1 preceding its levy. The following persons are exempted: Indians not taxed, insane, blind, deaf or dumb persons, those who have lost a hand or foot, those permanently disabled and all disabled veterans of foreign wars, where such disability is 40% or more. Poll tax may be paid any time between October 1 and February 1; poll tax receipt to be given even if other taxes unpaid. Anyone exempt from poll tax may vote on obtaining certificate of exemption from County Tax Collector. May pay poll tax by mail or in person, but in paying must complete forms with information about age, residence, race, etc. Aliens receive special receipt.

ABSENTEE: Mail poll tax receipt to County Tax Collector to receive certificate for voting.

TRANSFER:

Address: In cities under 10,000, if move from one precinct or county to another, may vote on presentation of poll tax receipt. In cities over 10,000, present tax receipt or certificate of exemption to Tax Collector not less than 4 days before election or primary; Collector then adds voter's name to list of qualified voters.

Name: No provision found.

Party Affiliation: Voter becomes qualified member of political party by voting in party primary; affiliation lasts until end of poll tax period.

UTAH

PERSONAL: Apply to Registration Agent on 1st, 3rd and 4th Tuesdays of August, and 4th, 3rd and 1st Tuesdays and, in presidential years, the 1st Wednesday before general election.

If no Registration Agent in elector's own district, may with due proof of identity register in another district in county; in this case, obtain registration certificate.

Special Provision: If absent from county during regular registration days, register at County Clerk's office except for 10 days before any election.

ABSENTEE: Physically disabled voter request official form from County Clerk; execute and return with certificate of physical disability to Clerk any time except 10 days before election.

TRANSFER:

Address: If move from one district to another within county before election day, apply to Registration Agent in former district any time up to and including Saturday before election and request removal of name from official register. Registration Agent will provide Registry Transfer Certificate which will entitle elector to be registered in new district any time up to and including Saturday before election. In no event may voter return and vote in district from which he has moved.

Name: No provision found.

Party Affiliation: No provision found; party affiliation not listed on registration record.

VERMONT

PERSONAL: Voter must obtain "approbation" of Board of Civil Authority of town in which he resides. Town Clerk records name of person taking freeman's oath and date when taken and upon request shall certify to same. Check-list of town is furnished in December in even-numbered years by Town Clerk to Secretary of State; voter's name must be on check-list before he can vote. Hearings to revise check-list are held by Board of Civil Authority 30 days before every election.

ABSENTEE: No provision found.

TRANSFER:
Address: If temporarily absent from resident town, file declaration of intention to return to residence in Town Clerk's office at least 3 months before general election. If move from one town to another within 60 days of general election, may retain former residence for voting purposes in such election by filing declaration of intention with Town Clerk before departure.
Name: No provision found.
Party Affiliation: No provision found.

VIRGINIA
PERSONAL: Apply to County, City or Town Registrar any time up to 30 days before election. Payment of poll tax is voting requisite; voting lists are compiled from poll tax lists.
ABSENTEE: No provision.
TRANSFER:
Address: If move from one election district to another within same county or city, apply in writing or in person to Registrar of former precinct requesting Certificate of Registration. Present Certificate to Registrar of new election district. If change from one election district to another in town of less than 2,500, register on election day by presenting Certificate of Transfer. If transfer to another city or county, obtain in person or in writing Certificate of Registration any time from Registrar of former election district and present to new Registrar.
Name: Apply in writing to Registrar.
Party Affiliation: No provision found.

WASHINGTON
PERSONAL: Apply to City Clerk or to County Auditor in rural areas any time except 30 days before election. Registration closed during this 30-day period except for 15 days during which elector may make minor registration changes.
ABSENTEE: No provision found.
TRANSFER:
Address: Apply in person or by mail to City Clerk to change address from one place to another in same city or town, or to County Auditor if move from one rural precinct to another within county. Re-register and authorize cancellation of former registration if move from one county to another.
Name: Re-register.
Party Affiliation: Party affiliation not listed on registration.

WEST VIRGINIA
PERSONAL: Apply to Clerk of County Court any time except 30 days before election.
ABSENTEE: Apply by mail to Clerk of County Court if absent from state due to occupation or any necessary cause.
TRANSFER:
Address: If move within county, apply any time except 30 days

before election in person or in writing on official form to Clerk of County Court. If move when registration closed, vote in former precinct.

Name: Re-register in person or by mail.

Party Affiliation: No provision found.

WISCONSIN

PERSONAL: Apply to Clerk of municipality (or Board of Election Commissioners in Milwaukee) any time except after 5 P.M. on 2nd Wednesday before election. During 10 days before election if not registered may present affidavit to Clerk of municipality stating one is qualified to vote; affidavit must be substantiated by affidavits of 2 freeholders. If affidavit is in order, elector allowed to vote.

ABSENTEE: If more than 50 miles away from legal residence write to Clerk of municipality for registration affidavits; complete, have notarized, and return to Clerk before close of last registration day.

TRANSFER:

Address: If move within municipality, apply in person or in writing to Clerk (or Board of Election Commissioners in Milwaukee).

Name: No provision found.

Party Affiliation: No provision found.

WYOMING

PERSONAL: Apply to Registry Agent in election district or to City, Town or County Clerk any time except the 15 days before and 10 days after any general or special election. Register with Judges of Election at polling place for primary.

ABSENTEE: If absent and unable to appear in person to register, apply not less than 30 days before election to County Clerk for Oath of Registration. Oath must be notarized and returned not less than 15 days before election.

TRANSFER:

Address: If move from one precinct to another within same county, apply in writing to County Clerk. If move from one county to another, re-register.

Name: No provision found.

Party Affiliation: Participation in primary constitutes declaration of party affiliation. If vote in one primary, cannot change party for 2 years. If challenged, must swear that change is in good faith; enrollment will then be changed.

CHART IV

CIVILIAN ABSENTEE VOTING PROVISIONS

NOTE: In all states an affidavit, sworn to before a notary public or other officer legally authorized to administer oaths, must accompany the absentee ballot.

ALABAMA
ABSENTEE VOTER: Elector on official list of qualified voters, whose business or occupation regularly requires his absence from county.

PROCEDURE: Apply in person not more than 20 nor less than 5 days before election to Register of county or his deputy. Receive "duplicate absentee ballot" including carbon paper; mark ballot at office of Register.

ALASKA
ABSENTEE VOTER: Elector unavoidably absent from home on election day and more than 2 miles distant from regular voting place.

PROCEDURE: Apply in person to Commissioner of recording district not more than 90 days nor less than 1 day before election. Or if live 5 miles distant from office of Commissioner, apply to Postmaster who is authorized to issue ballots, administer oath and execute certificate. Or apply in writing to Commissioner not more than 90 nor less than 4 days before election, except physically disabled voter may apply in writing up to and on election day provided application accompanied by physician's letter. Mail ballot to Clerk of District Court by election day. (Postmark is evidence of mailing date.)

ARIZONA
ABSENTEE VOTER: Elector absent from county, or physically disabled (physician's certificate required), or unable to attend polls because of tenets of religion.

PROCEDURE: Request in person or in writing Application for Ballot form from County Recorder within 30 days before Saturday before election. Execute application form in duplicate and return to Recorder. Return ballot before 6 P.M. on election day, unless special arrangements made in case of sudden illness of elector. Elector may also vote in person at County Recorder's office any time after absentee ballots are available.

ARKANSAS
ABSENTEE VOTER: Elector unavoidably absent because of duties, occupation or business, or unable to go to polls because of illness or physical disability, or employee of railroad, traveling salesman, or student of any college of the state.

PROCEDURE: Apply in person or in writing to County Clerk

not earlier than 15 days (20 days if applicant is outside United States) nor later than 1 day before election; or applicant or member of his immediate family may apply to County Clerk not later than 1:30 P.M. election day. Return ballot by mail or through agent by 6:30 P.M. election day. Elector may also cast ballot in person with County Clerk any time between 15th day before election and 6:30 P.M. election day.

CALIFORNIA

ABSENTEE VOTER: Elector absent from precinct or unable to go to polls because of physical disability or tenets of religion or because attendance at religious service is required, or who resides within precinct owned or controlled by United States or resides more than 10 miles from nearest polling place.

PROCEDURE: Apply in writing to County Clerk not more than 20 nor less than 5 days before election. Return ballot to Clerk or Registrar of Voters within 9 days after election. Or vote in person at office of County, Municipal or District Clerk any day before election. If because of sudden illness or disability voter cannot go to polls, request ballot in writing; County Clerk will give ballot to authorized representative who presents doctor's letter stating that voter is patient in hospital, sanitorium, or nursing home.

COLORADO

ABSENTEE VOTER: Elector absent from county, or absent by reason of work or nature of employment, or ill or physically disabled, or unable to attend polls because of religious beliefs.

PROCEDURE: May vote in person at special polling places established for "absent voters" in city or town or county seat not earlier than 15 days nor later than 12 noon on Saturday before election. Or apply in person or in writing to County Clerk (or to Election Commission if resident of Denver) not earlier than 90 days nor later than 12 noon on Saturday before election. Return ballot in person or by mail to County Clerk or Election Commission by 5 P.M. election day.

CONNECTICUT

ABSENTEE VOTER: Elector absent from state or ill or physically disabled.

PROCEDURE: No absentee voting in primaries. Apply in person or by mail on official form to Town, City or Borough Clerk any time within 2 months of election. Return ballot to Clerk by 6 P.M. of day before election.

Special Provision: Qualified elector who moves to another state may vote by absentee ballot for presidential electors in town from which he moved for 24 months after time he moved if he has not become elector in another state. Apply in writing to Town Clerk not more than 2 months before election for "Absentee Presidential Elector Ballot".

DELAWARE

ABSENTEE VOTER: Elector unable to go to polls because he is in public service of United States or state of Delaware, or because of business or occupation, or personal sickness or disability. File affidavit with Department of Elections in county not more than 30 days before election; if claim physical disability, present affidavit by licensed physician; if claim nature of business prevents attendance at polls, present affidavit from employer, or if self-employed sign own affidavit.

PROCEDURE: No absentee voting in primaries. Apply in person or through representative to County Department of Elections up to 5 P.M. of day before general election. Apply in writing to Department of Elections not more than 60 nor less than 3 days before general election. Return ballot to Department of Elections before 12 noon of election day.

FLORIDA

ABSENTEE VOTER: Elector absent from county on election day or physically disabled or unable to go to polls because of tenets of religion.

PROCEDURE: Apply in person or by mail on official blank to Supervisor of Registration in county any time from 45th day to 5 P.M. of 5th day before election. (Person unable to vote because of religious tenets must apply in person.) Return ballot to Supervisor by 5 P.M. of day before election.

GEORGIA

ABSENTEE VOTER: Elector required to be absent from city, county, ward or district, or physically disabled (physician's certificate required).

PROCEDURE: Voter or member of family must give written notice of intention to vote by mail not less than 5 nor more than 60 days before election. Apply by letter to County Registrars. Voter may mark ballot in presence of Postmaster or notary public. Return ballot immediately after marking.

HAWAII

ABSENTEE VOTER: Elector absent from island of residence on election day.

PROCEDURE: Apply in person or in writing to County Clerk not more than 20 nor less than 10 days before election. Return ballot to County Clerk by day before election. Elector who will be absent from county or district on election day may cast ballot in person at office of County Clerk or District Magistrate during 10 days before election.

Special provision: Patients in hospitals, physically disabled confined to home, and voters in county of Kalawao who are in settlement for Hansen's disease should check local regulations.

IDAHO

ABSENTEE VOTER: Elector absent from precinct on election

day or physically disabled or blind.

PROCEDURE: Apply in person or by mail to County Auditor or City Clerk. Return ballot by registered mail not later than 1 day before election.

ILLINOIS

ABSENTEE VOTER: Elector absent from county in course of business or duties, or physically disabled (physician's or practitioner's certificate required).

PROCEDURE: Apply in person or writing on official blank to County Clerk or to Board of Election Commissioners in Chicago. Apply in writing not more than 30 nor less than 5 days before election; apply in person up to 3 days before election. Return ballot by mail or in person in time for delivery to proper polling place before polls close.

INDIANA

ABSENTEE VOTER: Elector absent because of business or profession or physical infirmity (physician's or practitioner's certificate required) or attendance at school, college, university or other institution of learning as student or spouse of student, or absent because of service as member of an election board.

PROCEDURE: Apply to Clerk of Circuit Court of County in person or by mail not more than 60 days before general or city election nor more than 30 days before primary nor later than Saturday next prior to any election. Application must be signed and sworn to by 2 legal, resident freehold voters of elector's precinct. Return ballot by election day.

IOWA

ABSENTEE VOTER: Elector absent from county on business or other necessary travel, or physically disabled or ill.

PROCEDURE: Apply in person or in writing to County Auditor or City or Town Clerk within 20 days before election. Return ballot at least 1 day before election.

KANSAS

ABSENTEE VOTER: Elector absent from state or ill or physically disabled.

PROCEDURE: If physically disabled, apply not more than 25 days nor later than Thursday before election to County Clerk, Election Commissioner or City Clerk. (Physician's certificate required.) Ballot need *not* be notarized; must be returned by 9 A.M. Monday before election. Otherwise apply to County Clerk between April 1 in general election year and the last Thursday before primary or between September 1 and the last Thursday before general election. Or on Friday, Saturday and until 12 noon on Monday before any election, file affidavit with County Clerk stating elector will be absent. Elector will receive ballot which must be returned before 1 P.M. on Monday before election.

KENTUCKY
ABSENTEE VOTER: Elector absent from county in course of business or duties on election day.
PROCEDURE: Apply in person or in writing on official form to Clerk of County Court any time up to 10 days before election. Return ballot to Clerk before close of polls.

LOUISIANA
ABSENTEE VOTER: Elector absent from parish on election day.
PROCEDURE: Apply in person to Clerk of District Court of parish not more than 10 nor less than 2 days before election. In parish of Orleans apply to Civil Sheriff. Voter marks ballot in presence of election officer.

MAINE
ABSENTEE VOTER: Elector absent because of business or physical disability (physician's certificate required) or unable to go to polls for religious reasons.
PROCEDURE: Apply in writing in "seasonable time" to City or Town Clerk. Return ballot by mail or in person by close of polls.

MARYLAND
ABSENTEE VOTER: Elector unavoidably absent from state or any disabled or ill voter who is absent from ward or district on election day. (If claim illness, file physician's certificate at least 10 days before election.)
PROCEDURE: Apply in writing on official form to City or County Board of Supervisors of Election at least 20 days before election. Return ballot by close of polls.

MASSACHUSETTS
ABSENTEE VOTER: Elector absent due to business or any other reason, or physically disabled. (Certificate of physician, attending registered nurse, hospital superintendent or practitioner required.)
PROCEDURE: No absentee voting in primaries. Apply in writing, preferably on official form, or in person to Secretary of Commonwealth or to City or Town Clerk any time before election. Mail ballot by election day. Postmark is evidence of mailing time. Agent may return ballot for voter on high seas in prosecution of business of fishing or as mariner.

MICHIGAN
ABSENTEE VOTER: Elector absent from township or physically disabled or unable to go to polls because of tenets of religion. Or student at institution of learning or teacher in Michigan public schools, or member of citizens' military or naval training camp, or member of legislature in attendance at any session, or his immediate family, or commercial traveler, or elector employed upon or in operation of railroad trains in the state, or sailor employed on Great Lakes or in coastwise trade.

Former Michigan residents living in District of Columbia also may cast absentee ballot.

PROCEDURE: Apply in person or by mail on official form to City or Town Clerk any time between 75th day and 2 P.M. of Saturday before election. Return ballot to Clerk in time for delivery to proper polling place before polls close.

MINNESOTA

ABSENTEE VOTER: Elector absent from district or ill or physically disabled or unable to go to polls because of religious discipline or observance of religious holiday.

PROCEDURE: Apply to County Auditor not earlier than 45 days nor later than 1 day before election. Return ballot to County Auditor by election day.

MISSISSIPPI

ABSENTEE VOTER: Elector who is driver, operator or crewman on common carrier in interstate commerce (trains, buses, trucks, airplanes, and sea-going ships and vessels) may vote *in absentia*, but cannot register *in absentia*.

PROCEDURE: Must vote absentee ballot in person at office of Circuit Clerk, or at City Clerk's office in case of municipal election, not more than 10 nor less than 2 days before election.

MISSOURI

ABSENTEE VOTER: Elector absent from county, ill or physically disabled. (Physician's or practitioner's certificate required.)

PROCEDURE: Apply by mail on official blank or in letter or in person to County Clerk or to Board of Election Commissioners during 30 days before and up to 6 P.M. on day before election. Return ballot by 6 P.M. of day after election. Must be postmarked no later than date of election.

MONTANA

ABSENTEE VOTER: Elector absent from county or physically disabled. (Physician's certificate required.)

PROCEDURE: Apply on official form to County Clerk during 45 days before election. Return ballot in time for delivery to polling place before polls close. May vote in person at County Clerk's office any time after official ballots are printed.

NEBRASKA

ABSENTEE VOTER: Elector absent from county or physically disabled. (Physician's certificate required.)

PROCEDURE: Apply in writing to County Clerk or Election Commissioner in Douglas and Lancaster counties not more than 90 nor less than 2 days before election. Disabled voter may apply in writing through agent not earlier than 10 days nor later than 4 P.M. on day before election. Must submit physician's certificate that elector is *compos mentis*, not afflicted with contagious disease or under quarantine, and that state of health makes it unwise for him to go to polls. Return ballot not later than midnight of day before election; ballot returned by mail must bear postmark before midnight of day before election. May vote in person before County Clerk or Election Commissioner up to 2 clear days before election.

NEVADA
ABSENTEE VOTER: Elector absent because of vocation, business or other unavoidable cause, or illness or physical disability, and spouse and dependents of such voter in most instances.

PROCEDURE: If within United States, apply in person or in writing to County Clerk not more than 90 nor less than 5 days before election. If outside United States apply not more than 90 nor less than 10 days before election. Return ballot to County Clerk before close of polls.

Mailing Precincts: Precincts with not more than 20 voters voting in general election are declared mailing precincts. Residents of such precincts apply in person or by mail to County Clerk for official mailing ballot not more than 30 nor less than 15 days before election. Return ballot to County Clerk 10 days before election. Or resident of mailing precinct may mark ballot in person in presence of County Clerk.

NEW HAMPSHIRE
ABSENTEE VOTER: Elector absent from place of voting or physically disabled.

PROCEDURE: No absentee voting in primaries. Apply in writing on official form or in letter or in person to City or Town Clerk any time before election. Return ballot to Clerk in time for delivery to Moderator at proper polling place before close of polls.

NEW JERSEY
ABSENTEE VOTER: Elector absent *outside* the state on election day, or elector *within* the state but unable to go to polls because of illness or physical disability. (Physician's certificate required.)

PROCEDURE: Apply in writing to County Clerk (for state and county elections) up to 8 days before election. Return ballot to County Clerk before close of polls.

NEW MEXICO: No provision.

NEW YORK
ABSENTEE VOTER: Elector unavoidably absent from residence because he is inmate of veterans' bureau hospital (certificate from hospital officer required), or absent from county because of duties, occupation, business or responsibilities as student, superintendent or teacher in institution of learning located outside county, or spouse or dependent of such persons, or ill or physically disabled. (Physician's certificate required.)

PROCEDURE: No absentee voting in primaries. Apply in person

or by mail to Board of Elections 30 to 7 days before general election. Affidavit attesting to facts of absence is required except for those who are ill or physically disabled. In areas where permanent personal registration is in effect, voter classified as "Hospitalized Veteran" or "Hospitalized Veteran's Relative" will be sent absentee ballot without application. Return ballot by 5 P.M. Friday before election.

NORTH CAROLINA

ABSENTEE VOTER: Elector absent from county or ill or physically disabled.

PROCEDURE: No absentee voting in primaries. Apply in person or through member of family or in writing on official form to Chairman of County Board of Elections not more than 30 nor less than 2 days before election. Return ballot to Chairman by 3 P.M. election day.

NORTH DAKOTA

ABSENTEE VOTER: Elector absent from county or physically disabled. (Certificate of hospital superintendent or physician required.)

PROCEDURE: Apply in person or in writing on official form to County Auditor any time within 30 days before election. Return ballot in time for delivery to proper polling place before polls close. May vote in person before leaving the county; apply to County Auditor.

OHIO

ABSENTEE VOTER: Elector unavoidably absent and more than 10 miles from polling place on election day or physically disabled or ill. (Physician's certificate required.)

PROCEDURE: Apply in writing on official form to Clerk of County Board of Elections. If within United States, apply not more than 30 nor less than 5 days before election; if outside United States, apply no earlier than 60 days nor later than 4 P.M. of 5th day before election. Return ballot by mail not later than 12 noon of 4th day before election. May also cast absentee ballot in person at Board of Elections before election day.

OKLAHOMA

ABSENTEE VOTER: Elector absent from county on election day or physically incapacitated through accident or illness. (The latter must be attested to before 2 witnesses.)

PROCEDURE: Apply in person or in writing on official form to Secretary of County Election Board not earlier than 30 days nor later than 5 P.M. on Friday before election. Application must be accompanied by proof of valid registration on form filled out and signed by applicant's Precinct Registrar. Return ballot to County Election Board by 5 P.M. Friday before election. If apply for ballot in person, must vote immediately.

OREGON
ABSENTEE VOTER: Elector absent from polling place or living more than 15 miles from his polling place or physically disabled. (Physician's or practitioner's certificate required.)

PROCEDURE: Apply in person or in writing to County or City Clerk not more than 60 nor less than 5 days before election. Ballot must either be notarized or attested to by 2 competent persons whose signatures and addresses must be signed. Return ballot before close of polls. Or mark ballot in person in Clerk's office before 5 P.M. of day before election.

PENNSYLVANIA
ABSENTEE VOTER: Any qualified elector unavoidably absent from county because of duties, business or occupation, or ill, or physically disabled.

PROCEDURE: Apply in person to Chief Clerk of County Board of Elections not more than 30 nor less than 7 days before election. If ill or physically disabled, or if expect to be absent during 30 days preceding election, apply in writing to Chief Clerk. Mark ballot in secret, sign affidavit and have signature witnessed by subscribing witness. Mail ballot by election day (postmark is proof of mailing date). Ballot must reach County Board of Elections by 10 A.M. of second Friday following election.

RHODE ISLAND
ABSENTEE VOTER: Elector absent from state or because of old age, physical disability, illness or other physical infirmities unable to vote in person.

PROCEDURE: No absentee voting in primaries. Obtain from Secretary of State or local election board affidavit form for application for absentee ballot. Complete affidavit, have it notarized or sworn to before 2 witnesses and deliver in person or by mail to Secretary of State by 5 P.M. on 14th day before election. Ballots must be mailed from outside Rhode Island (postmark is considered evidence of place of mailing) except for physically disabled voter, casting a "shut-in" ballot, who may cast ballot within state. Return ballot to State Board of Elections by 9 P.M. election day. Patients in hospitals and convalescent homes may cast "shut-in" ballot at hospital during 5 days before election. Election supervisors visit hospitals for this purpose.

SOUTH CAROLINA: No provision.

SOUTH DAKOTA
ABSENTEE VOTER: Elector absent from precinct or ill or physically disabled.

PROCEDURE: Apply in person or in writing to County or City Auditor or Town Clerk any time after official ballots available. Return ballot to Superintendent of Election Board of precinct by mail or in person by election day. May vote in person during 15 days before election in presence of election official.

TENNESSEE

ABSENTEE VOTER: Elector (or wife accompanying him) absent from county because of business, occupation, health, education or travel, or elector who is ill or physically disabled. (Physician's certificate required.)

PROCEDURE: Apply in person or in writing to County Commissioner of Elections not more than 40 nor less than 5 days before election if voter is within United States and not more than 90 nor less than 20 days before election if voter is outside United States. Return ballot by registered mail to Commissioner by close of polls or voter may obtain absentee ballot from Commissioner and vote in person.

TEXAS

ABSENTEE VOTER: Elector absent from county at time of applying for absentee ballot and to be absent during remainder of period for absentee voting in person, or ill or physically disabled. (Physician's or practitioner's certificate required.)

PROCEDURE: Apply in writing to County Clerk not more than 20 nor less than 3 days before election. Send poll tax receipt or exemption certificate or affidavit that they have been lost or mislaid. Must be postmarked from point outside county. Return ballot to County Clerk before 1 P.M. election day or elector may vote in person at office of County Clerk any time between 20th and 3rd day before election.

UTAH

ABSENTEE VOTER: Elector absent from county and not within 20 miles of election district on election day or physically disabled. (Physician's certificate required.)

PROCEDURE: Apply in person or by mail on official blank to County Clerk within 30 days before election. Return ballot in time for delivery to polling place by close of polls.

VERMONT

ABSENTEE VOTER: Elector in town but unable to go to polls because of illness, injury or other disability, or because of religious principles, or necessarily absent from legal residence.

PROCEDURE: Apply in writing to Town Clerk any time up to 9 P.M. on 4th day before election, but application deadline waived in certain emergency circumstances. Return ballot to Town Clerk by election day. May vote in person before Town Clerk up to 9 P.M. on 4th day before election. Pairs of election officials may visit home of physically disabled voter on election day and he may cast absentee ballot.

VIRGINIA

ABSENTEE VOTER: Elector absent in regular and orderly course of profession, occupation or other personal affairs, or on vacation or as student at school or physically disabled.

98

PROCEDURE: Apply in person or by mail to Registrar of precinct not more than 60 nor less than 8 days before election if in United States; if outside United States apply not more than 90 nor less than 10 days before election. Include necessary postage for registering and sending ballot from Electoral Board and statement made before at least 1 witness that reasons cited for absentee voting are valid. Return ballot by registered or certified mail to Board in time for delivery to polling place by close of polls.

WASHINGTON

ABSENTEE VOTER: Elector absent from precinct or unable to vote due to physical disability or religious tenets.

PROCEDURE: Apply in person or by mail or by messenger to County Auditor or City Clerk within 45 days before election for absentee voter's certificate. Present certificate in person or by mail to election officer issuing ballots for election any time before election day.

WEST VIRGINIA

ABSENTEE VOTER: Elector absent because of employment, business or other unavoidable causes, or physical disability. (Physician's certificate required.)

PROCEDURE: Apply in person or by mail on official form to Clerk of Circuit Court not more than 30 nor less than 10 days before election. Return ballot by registered mail or deliver in person to Clerk of Circuit Court in time for delivery to Election Commissioners before close of polls. May vote in person not more than 10 nor less than 4 days before election.

WISCONSIN

ABSENTEE VOTER: Elector absent for any reason, or unable to go to polls because of illness, physical disability or religious reasons.

PROCEDURE: Apply in person or in writing to County, City, Village, or Town Clerk, or in cities of the first class to Secretary of Board of Election Commissioners. Apply by mail not more than 60 nor less than 3 days before election; apply in person not later than day before election. Return ballot by mail or in person to Clerk in time for delivery to proper precinct before close of polls.

WYOMING

ABSENTEE VOTER: Elector absent from county, or patient in hospital within county or physically disabled.

PROCEDURE: Apply in person or by mail to County, City or Town Clerk within 30 days before election or within 10 days if elector is patient in hospital or is physically disabled. Return ballot in person or by mail to Clerk in time for delivery to precinct before polls close.

INDEX